Part 1

Introduction

The life of Jane Austen

Jane Austen was born in December 1775, the seventh of eight children of George Austen, a Church of England clergymen, and his wife Cassandra, the daughter of another clergyman – both families had many Church and University connections. The Austens, a happy, well-educated and affectionate family, lived at the rectory in the parish of Steventon in Hampshire from 1764 to 1801 when George Austen retired. Two of Jane Austen's brothers became clergymen (one having previously been a banker). Another inherited land in Kent and Hampshire. Two had distinguished careers in the British Navy, one becoming Commander of the Fleet, the other Commander-in-Chief of the East India Station. As was usual at the time, the daughters did not have careers, but stayed at home, except for visits to friends. Jane and her sister Cassandra went to small boarding-schools when very young, but after the age of eleven were educated at home. They read widely in eighteenth-century fiction, played the piano and learnt Italian and French. Jane and Cassandra were devoted to each other, and much of our information about Jane's life and opinions comes from her letters written to Cassandra whenever either was away from home. Jane Austen went to stay for long periods with friends in the counties of Hampshire, Kent, Gloucestershire, Berkshire and Surrey, and also in London. At home, the Austens were popular in their neighbourhood, and accepted by some aristocratic families and 'landed gentry'; they attended many balls, parties and entertainments.

Jane Austen began to write stories and sketches for her family at the age of twelve. By 1795 she had written a comic *History of the World*; an unfinished novel, *Catherine*; and two epistolary novels, *Lady Susan* and *Elinor and Marianne*, which she was later to rewrite as *Sense and Sensibility*. In 1797 she started *First Impressions*, the first draft of *Pride and Prejudice*, and in 1798 *Susan*, which was published after her death as *Northanger Abbey*.

In 1801 the Austen family moved to Bath, the fashionable resort in the West of England, famous for its healing spa waters. Jane Austen is reputed to have met a young man during a visit to Devonshire in 1802 to whom she was greatly attracted, but he died in 1803. She was also proposed to in 1803 by a wealthy Hampshire landowner; she accepted, but retracted her acceptance the following morning. She never married, but had a full social life with many friends, and a large family circle, with numerous nieces and nephews to whom she was very close – in particular her niece Anna, an aspiring novelist with whom she corresponded. After a break in writing from 1801 to 1804, she began *The Watsons*, a novel which she never finished, probably because of the death of her father in 1805.

In 1807 Jane Austen, her sister Cassandra and their mother moved to Southampton, a large seaport, and in 1809 back to Hampshire to the village of Chawton. It was at Chawton Cottage that she wrote most of her completed novels. In November 1811 her first published novel, *Sense and Sensibility*, appeared, and was very successful. *Pride and Prejudice* was published in January 1813, *Mansfield Park* in May 1814 and *Emma* very early in 1816. She finished *Persuasion* in July 1816, and began *Sanditon* in 1817, but after two months became too ill to finish it. Her health continued to decline until July of that year when she died, aged only forty-two, after only five years as a successful writer. *Northanger Abbey* and *Persuasion* were published in 1818. So the six great novels for which she is remembered all appeared within seven years. They were all published anonymously, and written in secret, though it became known that she was the author, and she was officially requested to dedicate *Emma* to the Prince Regent (against her own wishes).

Historical background

The period of Jane Austen's life (1775–1817) was one of great turmoil in world affairs. The French Revolution of 1789 was the starting point for many revolutionary movements throughout the world; and although Britain did not have a revolution, she was actively engaged in wars and insurrections all over the world. In 1793 France declared war on her, and from then until just before Jane Austen's death, the two countries were almost continually at war under their great commanders, Napoleon and Wellington. Napoleon was crowned Emperor in 1804, defeated the Austrians in 1805; in the same year Admiral Nelson defeated the French Fleet at Trafalgar. From 1808 to 1814, Britain was also fighting the Peninsular War against the French in Spain and Portugal. The wars against Napoleon culminated in the Battle of Waterloo in 1815 when Wellington and the British, with the help of Blucher and the Prussians, defeated the French under Napoleon; Louis XVIII was restored to the throne of France, and Napoleon was exiled to Saint Helena.

The Napoleonic wars were not the only military concerns of the British: in 1798 the Irish Rebellion had to be put down; two years later the Act of Union between Great Britain and Ireland was passed, making

Ireland part of Great Britain. From 1799 onwards, Britain was also fighting the Mahratta wars in India.

The American War of Independence had come to an end in 1783, when Britain lost America as a colony: the newly independent country declared war on Britain in 1812, the war continuing until 1814. And Britain had many lesser engagements elsewhere: in 1807 Wellington wrote to the Prime Minister that he was 'ready to set out for any part of the world at a moment's notice', and indeed in that year alone, British forces had engagements in Brazil, Egypt, Sweden and Venezuela.

At home, George III had been king since 1760; in 1810 he became mentally deranged and the Regency Bill of 1811 declared his son (later George IV) ruler in his place. As Prince Regent, George IV was politically untrustworthy, as a man he was gross and licentious, but he was remarkable as a leader in fashion and taste. He was pre-eminent in establishing the very distinctive style of his age in architecture, landscape, dress and entertainment. Houses and estates were replanned by 'improvers' such as Humphrey Repton, on 'picturesque' rather than formal principles: 'improvements' are frequently discussed in *Mansfield Park*. Architecture, after the regularity of the classical style of the preceding age, became ornate and fanciful – 'Regency Gothic' – or elaborately 'rustic', or oriental, like the Brighton Pavilion, built for the Prince Regent, with its domes, minarets and Chinese furniture and decorations. With his friend 'Beau' Brummell he set an extremely elegant style of dress for men; not multicoloured and dandyish, but dark and severe; women wore neo-classic clothes, typically a white muslin dress, simple and flowing, with a high feather headress or turban for grand occasions, or the more usual bonnet for every day. The Prince Regent popularised the idea of staying at seaside resorts such as Weymouth and Brighton, or at fashionable spas such as Bath, all of which appear in Jane Austen's novels. Other places of entertainment with which Jane Austen was familiar through her visits to London included the many theatres; Ranelagh Gardens and Vauxhall Gardens, pleasure gardens for strolling, amusements and refreshments; Almack's Club, the summit of London 'Society', for dancing; and a host of other diversions such as music and firework displays on the River Thames.

Jane Austen's letters are full of details about this background, both international and national. Her naval brothers were actively engaged in the Napoleonic wars, she had friends and relatives concerned in the Indian uprisings, in the war with America, in the West Indies, even killed in the French revolution, and all of these places and matters are mentioned in her letters. So are the clothes that she and other people wore. But her novels are not meant to be histories or fashion plates; in them one only becomes aware of background according to the characters' awareness of it. She will not, for example, give a top-to-toe description of a woman's dress, but from conversation we gather, say, that Fanny Price looks charming in the white gown with 'glossy spots' bought for her by Sir Thomas for Maria's wedding (*Mansfield Park*, Chapter 23). Because all the characters are interested in 'improvements', we learn about their houses and estates; Fanny is vividly conscious of the details of Sotherton (Chapters 9–10) and of the park at Mansfield on her return in spring (Chapter 46), so we receive very clear impressions of them. But unless it was necessary for such purposes, Jane Austen, writing for her contemporaries, avoided self-conscious descriptions of the background and 'current affairs'. She has been criticised for writing at the time of the Napoleonic Wars without mentioning them – except insofar as military preparations bring a regiment of militia to Meryton to provide dancing partners for the Bennet sisters in *Pride and Prejudice*. She was, however, intensively and exclusively concerned with the regiment's effect upon the social life of Meryton and the Bennets, and not at all with its effect upon the (unspecified) enemy. She was not eager to load her novels with topical references to events which, however historically important, did not impinge very much on daily life in provincial England, her special domain.

Literary background

Chronologically, Jane Austen's work stands between the neo-classical formality of the eighteenth century and the effusive, emotional Romanticism of the nineteenth century. It stands at the point where the 'Age of Reason' becomes the 'Age of Sensibility'. But she belongs to no 'school' of writers, and indeed the more her manner, style, or content resembles that of currently popular novelists, the more likely she is to be mocking them. The progress of the novel in England at the end of the eighteenth century did not correspond very closely to the pattern of other kinds of literature, and Jane Austen's style is very much more in tune with that of the poets and non-fictional prose writers of the mid-eighteenth century, the Augustan age. Although Jane Austen read the work of contemporary Romantic poets such as Robert Burns (1759–96), Sir Walter Scott (1771–1832) and Lord Byron (1788–1824), her style and content have much more in common with those of earlier poets such as Alexander Pope (1688–1744), or of essayists and critics such as Joseph Addison (1672–1719) or Samuel Johnson (1709–84). Their extreme formality of style, their balanced sentences, their carefully constructed sequences can still be traced in her prose; their advocation of moderation in all things, their morality, their satirical detachment are echoed in her manner.

The English novel, at the time when Jane Austen was writing, was still in the exciting grip of the Gothic. The Gothic romance was introduced to English literature by Horace Walpole (1717–97) with *The Castle of Otranto* (1765); it rejoiced in, or rather agonised over, picturesque horror, magic, superstition, murder and love, against a backdrop of sinister forests and gloomy mediaeval castles. There were some variations in background, all suitably exotic: William Beckford's *Vathek* (1786) was set in the mysterious East, Mrs Radcliffe's *The Mysteries of Udolpho* (1794) in sixteenth-century France and Italy; and abbeys and monasteries abounded, as for instance in Mrs Radcliffe's *The Italian* (1797), or in Matthew Gregory Lewis's *The Monk* (1795). These and many others brought the supernatural, diabolism, terror, and romance to the library tables of the fashionable.

Another vein of novel-writing was pursued by contemporary women writers, notably Fanny Burney (1752–1840) and Maria Edgeworth (1767–1849). Both wrote novels of 'manners'. Fanny Burney's *Evelina* (1778), written in letter form, shows the introduction of a young girl into London society; Maria Edgeworth's *Helen* and *Belinda* also show leisured society (at a more aristocratic level than Jane Austen does), but are neither as original nor as good as her *Castle Rackrent* (1800) which describes Irish life over several generations, as recounted by a peasant, Thady Quirk, in his own dialect. This third vein, the regional one, was to continue well into the nineteenth century. Sir Walter Scott published Scottish ballads (*Minstrelsy of the Scottish Border*) in 1802–3, wrote his first novel, *Waverley*, in 1814, and for the rest of Jane Austen's lifetime continued to write highly coloured romantic novels concerned with Scottish history and customs.

There are echoes of these three kinds of novel in Jane Austen's work. She makes fun of the Gothic novel and its conventions (especially in *Northanger Abbey*, a parody of the genre). Her close examination of social life has much in common with the novel of manners, and her novels could be said to be preserving in precise detail the manners and customs of provincial England. But Jane Austen differs from all her contemporaries in the subtlety of her characterisation, in the depth of her irony, and in the individual tone of her narration.

Jane Austen's novels

Jane Austen wrote to her niece Anna, who wished to become a novelist: 'three or four families in a country village is the very thing to work on'; she also described 'the little bit (two inches wide) of ivory on which I work with so fine a brush, as produces little effect after much labour'. The scale of three or four families is that of all Jane Austen's novels; the little bit of ivory with a complex miniature painted upon it is a good image of her highly detailed depiction of them, though admirers of her work would say that she had laboured to great, not little, effect.

Jane Austen set her 'three or four families' in a rigid hierarchy within their country villages. At a time when the dividing lines between the aristocracy and the upper middle class, between the upper middle class and people in business or 'trade' were becoming blurred, she chose the middle class as a small, encompassable, but richly varied social span. Within it she showed a well-defined traditional order of birth, money and land which could only be upset at one's peril. She preaches the conventional pattern of life in the family and in society; the pattern of behaviour expected of one towards family, friends, acquaintances, admirers, superiors and inferiors. The lessons of her novels are not to do with morals, ethics or religion, but with behaviour. One must learn how to behave towards other people; the individual must learn how to fit into society. One of the ways of knowing how to behave is to see clearly: in *Sense and Sensibility*, Marianne Dashwood must abandon her sensibility, or undue emotional sensitivity, before she can behave properly. In *Pride and Prejudice*, Mr Darcy and Elizabeth Bennet must rid themselves, the one of his pride, the other of her prejudice, before they can behave appropriately towards each other and towards others. In *Emma*, the heroine must control her 'fancy', or fantasising imagination, before she can fit herself into real events instead of trying to mould people around her imaginings. In *Mansfield Park*, Fanny Price must reach maturity and self-knowledge, and take her proper place in society, before she can be united with Edmund Bertram, who for his part must recover from his infatuation for the unworthy Mary Crawford; no longer blinded by romantic illusion, he must open his eyes to the truth.

People can be blinded to real life by the preconceptions they have acquired from popular literature; and one of the ways in which Jane Austen represents the realities of life is by pointing out how different it is from what romantic literature would have us believe. From her earliest stories Jane Austen poked fun at the novel of sensibility. *Love and Freindship*, which she wrote at fourteen, is a parody of the sensational romantic novel; much later she wrote a fake synopsis of a novel bringing in all the romantic subjects and backgrounds that her reading and her acquaintances had suggested to her ('Plan of a Novel according to hints from various quarters', about 1816). Marianne Dashwood's sensibility, Emma's fancy, Elizabeth Bennet's prejudice, are ultimately derived from literature. But Jane Austen's funniest and most scathing attack on contemporary literature is *Northanger Abbey*, in which she turns the Gothic convention on its romantic head. Catherine Morland expects Northanger to be a 'real' Gothic Abbey, and is taken aback to find that it is bright and modern instead of mouldering and grim. Her 'passion for ancient edifices' and her 'visions of romance' make her either blind to real life, or disappointed in it. In the end, true love triumphs in a rather down-to-earth way and she marries Henry Tilney. Real life is found to be quite different from the expectations of the avid novel-reader. All of Janes Austen's novels end with the typical conclusion of the romantic novel, marriage for two or more of the main characters; the heroine of *Persuasion*, Anne Elliott, has been persuaded eight years ago to renounce her lover Frederick Wentworth, who reappears on the scene at the beginning of the novel; she is reunited with him at the end of it. But Jane Austen's way of arriving at the last-chapter marriages is not romantic; the happy end is achieved by sweeping away hypocrisy, literary notions, romantic illusions, snobbery and prejudice of all kinds, to arrive at truth, sincerity and a happy union, not just with one's beloved, but with the society in which one finds oneself.

A note on the text

Mansfield Park was begun about February 1811, and finished soon after June 1813. It was published in three volumes by Egerton of London in 1814, in a very small edition which sold out in six months. The second edition was published in 1816 by John Murray, also in three volumes. This is a much better-printed edition, and is the one that has been followed in all reprints. Of these, the finest modern edition of *Mansfield Park* is in the Oxford University Press series of the novels of Jane Austen, edited, with notes and appendices, by R. W. Chapman (1923, reprinted 12 times up to 1978). Although this is a single volume, it keeps to the three-volume scheme of chapter-numbers and pagination.

The text used in these Notes is that of the Penguin English Library edition, Penguin Books, Harmondsworth, first published in 1966 and reprinted many times. Here the chapter numbers are sequential, in one volume. The Penguin edition's Chapters 1–18 correspond to Volume I of the three-volume edition; Chapters 19–31 to Volume II (Chapters I–XIII); Chapters 32–48 to Volume III (Chapters I–XVII).

Part 2

Summaries
of MANSFIELD PARK

A general summary

Mansfield Park centres on the development of its heroine Fanny Price from a timid, passive girl to a mature and self-knowing woman. Fanny is inwardly 'shaped' by a house, Mansfield Park, which is the symbol of a cultivated, harmonious way of life. The most dramatic exterior happenings are those that disturb that way of life.

The principal themes woven around Fanny are, first, her integration into the world of Mansfield Park, which eventually entails a mental separation from her own family background. Second is her love for her cousin Edmund Bertram, impeded throughout the novel by his infatuation with a worldly heiress, Mary Crawford, and only reciprocated at the novel's end. Third is her courtship by Miss Crawford's brother Henry, steadfastly rejected by Fanny, and eventually ending when he elopes with her married cousin Maria Bertram.

We first meet Fanny Price at the age of ten, when she is taken into the house of her uncle and aunt, Sir Thomas and Lady Bertram. Lady Bertram's successful marriage contrasts with that of her sister, Fanny's mother, who has married a poor Lieutenant of Marines, now retired, lazy and inclined to drink. The remaining sister, Mrs Norris, is married to a clergyman. Awkward and frightened, Fanny meets her handsome, confident cousins Tom and Edmund, Maria and Julia. Edmund, who is to become a clergyman, is the only one who befriends and encourages her. After her initial terror, Fanny grows to love Mansfield Park.

When Fanny is eighteen, Sir Thomas has to go to the West Indies on business. Maria and Julia are in the midst of a busy social round, going to balls chaperoned by Mrs Norris, now widowed, while Fanny stays at home with the indolent Lady Bertram. Mrs Norris decides that Maria should marry Mr Rushworth, a rich but dull-witted young man with a fine house and estate, and they become unofficially engaged. During Sir Thomas's protracted absence, Henry and Mary Crawford come to stay at the parsonage with their half-sister Mrs Grant, whose husband Dr Grant became rector of the parish on Mr Norris's death. The Crawfords are rich and charming: Mrs Grant hopes that Henry will marry Julia Bertram, but Mary warns her that he is an incorrigible flirt. The two families become very friendly, with Julia and Maria (despite her engagement) both attracted by Henry Crawford, and Mary Crawford interested in Tom Bertram, who will inherit his father's title, money and estate. When he is away, however, she transfers her interest to Edmund, who, attracted first by her harp playing, then by her lively manner, falls in love with her. This attraction is noticed by Fanny, whom we already know to have tender feelings for Edmund; she is hurt when Edmund offers Miss Crawford the mare he had bought specially for Fanny to ride. Miss Crawford proves an excellent rider, keeps the mare longer and longer, and for several days she and Edmund go off to ride with the other young people, leaving Fanny with no exercise, and only her aunts for company. Edmund reproaches himself for this when he finds Fanny exhausted from running errands for her aunts; she is confused by his change from neglect to concern.

The two families plan a visit to Sotherton, Mr Rushworth's house, which he is anxious to 'improve'. Edmund ensures that Fanny, at first destined to be left behind, is included. Maria is vexed when Julia sits beside Henry Crawford on the driver's box, but grows more cheerful as they approach the splendid estate which will be hers on her marriage. Mr Rushworth and his mother show them the house; in the private chapel a joke made by Julia about Edmund performing the marriage ceremony for Maria and Mr Rushworth makes Mary Crawford realise for the first time that Edmund is to become a clergyman. She is taken aback, having already made several frivolous remarks about the clergy. In the garden, Miss Crawford and Edmund leave Fanny alone on a bench while they go to explore. Henry Crawford and Maria, after a flirtatious conversation, scramble past a locked gate into the park although Mr Rushworth has gone to get the key. Julia, cross, hurries after them. The whole party spends the day unsatisfactorily.

Tom's friend, John Yates, then comes to stay and fires all the young people with enthusiasm for acting; they plan a theatrical performance of a rather risqué play, *Lovers' Vows*, much to the dismay of Edmund and Fanny. Maria is given the leading role, and Julia, piqued that Henry Crawford does not propose her for it, flounces out, refusing to take part. Maria, showing a marked indifference to Mr Rushworth, rehearses incessantly with Mr Crawford. Mary Crawford persuades Edmund to play Anhalt the clergyman opposite her, despite his disapproval of the whole venture. The house is put into disarray; Sir Thomas's study is rearranged, scenery and stage are built. Lady Bertram is too lazy to disapprove, Mrs Norris too busy helping and interfering. Despite mounting pressure, Fanny refuses to take part, and watches the disintegration of the harmonious household and the indecorous behaviour of the actors; she is particularly disturbed when Edmund and Mary Crawford rehearse an outspoken scene together in her room. During the first rehearsal of all the cast, Sir Thomas returns unexpectedly.

Unaware of their dismay, Sir Thomas greets his family, finding Fanny much grown and much improved. It is not until he hears Mr Yates rehearsing that he finds out about the theatricals, to his horror. Deeply disappointed, particularly in Edmund, he has his house put back in order. The party disperses. Henry Crawford leaves abruptly, to Maria's chagrin; she had hoped that he would propose to her. Noticing her indifference to Mr Rushworth, Sir Thomas asks her if she really wishes to marry him, and she insists that she does. After the wedding, the couple goes away, accompanied by Julia. Fanny, as the only young woman left at home, is now more important and more confident. She becomes friendly with Mary Crawford. Henry Crawford resolves to make her fall in love with him, not knowing that she is protected by her feelings for Edmund. Her sailor brother William comes to stay, and Sir Thomas plans a 'coming out ball' for Fanny. Mary Crawford persuades her to accept a necklace (originally the gift of her brother Henry) to wear with an amber cross that William has given her. Fanny is much more pleased by a plainer gold chain bought for her by Edmund; she wears both. At the ball, Edmund and Mary Crawford disagree; she has continued to try to dissuade him from becoming a clergyman.

William goes back to sea. Mary Crawford becomes jealous of the friends with whom Edmund is staying before his ordination as a clergyman. Henry Crawford, now determined to marry Fanny, uses his influence to have William promoted, and then proposes to her. Despite her refusal, he perseveres: Sir Thomas and Mary Crawford press her to accept, and even Edmund regards the match as very suitable, and feels sure that Henry Crawford will prevail. He himself is on the point of proposing to Mary Crawford; she and her brother go to London.

Sir Thomas decides that Fanny should go to stay with her parents in Portsmouth; she finds a noisy, disorderly family and house, a slovenly mother and a coarse father. The only person who shows signs of sense or sensitivity is her sister Susan, whom she tries to guide and educate. Feeling very cut off from Mansfield society, Fanny has to rely only on letters for news. Henry Crawford unexpectedly visits her; though still refusing to marry him, she now thinks more highly of him. From letters she learns that Mary Crawford is becoming increasingly worldly; that Tom is dangerously ill (as a result of dissipation); that Edmund has not yet proposed to Mary Crawford. Sir Thomas cannot come at the end of the appointed two months to take Fanny back to Mansfield, which she now realises is her true home. Letters become increasingly disquieting as she learns of a rumour that Henry Crawford and Maria have eloped, then that the rumour is true, then that Julia has eloped with Mr Yates. Edmund comes to take Fanny home to Mansfield Park with Susan; he is distressed because Mary Crawford has taken Maria's elopement very lightly – he sees now that she is spoilt and corrupt. Fanny knows that she can comfort and help him and everybody at Mansfield Park.

In the final chapter we learn what happens to the characters in the aftermath of the elopements. Maria is divorced by Mr Rushworth, and lives for a time with Henry Crawford, but they part without marrying, she to live with Mrs Norris, inharmoniously. Mr Yates proves a more suitable husband for Julia than he appeared. Tom is restored to health and quiet living. Edmund, having thought he would never meet another woman like Mary Crawford, discovers that he loves Fanny. They marry; he eventually becomes the rector of Mansfield Park and they live happily in its parsonage. Fanny has taken her place in society.

Detailed summaries

Chapter 1

The three Misses Ward have made very different marriages, 'about thirty years ago'. Miss Maria Ward married Sir Thomas Bertram, a rich baronet with a beautiful house in Northamptonshire, Mansfield Park. Her elder sister married a poor clergyman, Mr Norris, whom Sir Thomas provided with a parish at Mansfield. The third sister made an imprudent secret marriage to a poor Lieutenant of Marines 'without education, fortune, or connections'; distance and social differences have caused a break between Mrs Price and her sisters. After eleven years, on the point of having her ninth baby, with a husband unable to continue in active service but inclined to drink and fond of company, Mrs Price writes to Lady Bertram for help. Mrs Norris suggests that she and the Bertrams should, between them, take the eldest girl, and despite Sir Thomas's doubts about the responsibilities entailed, 'the child', Fanny Price, is sent for. To the Bertrams' surprise, Mrs Norris now says that she cannot take any part in the child's upbringing, and leaves the Bertrams in sole charge.

NOTES AND GLOSSARY:

about thirty years ago: thirty years before the first edition would have been 1784

baronet: member of the lowest hereditary titled order. The title is the baronetcy; the baronet is addressed as 'Sir Thomas Bertram' or 'Sir Thomas'

Miss Ward, Miss Frances, Miss Maria: the eldest daughter living at home was called 'Miss . . .' with the surname, and the other daughters 'Miss . . . .' with the Christian name, with or without the surname ('Miss Frances', 'Miss Frances Ward')

interest: influence

Chapter 2

Fanny Price, at the age of ten, arrives in Northamptonshire from Portsmouth. Small and shy, she has a sweet voice and a pretty face; she is a little awkward but not vulgar (as might have been feared from her background). She is terrified of Sir Thomas, of Lady Bertram, of their two tall, good-humoured sons, Tom and Edmund (seventeen and sixteen), and of their handsome, self-confident daughters, Maria and Julia (thirteen and twelve). She grows 'more comfortable' after her cousin Edmund finds her crying, discovers that she misses her family, and gives her paper to write to her favourite brother William. Maria and Julia, encouraged by Mrs Norris, consider her ill-educated and lacking in the accomplishments upon which they pride themselves: Edmund sees that she is clever, encourages her to read, and develops her taste. He is to be a clergyman; the extravagant Tom will inherit the title and estate. Sir Thomas continues to help the Prices, and invites William to spend a week at Mansfield Park.

NOTES AND GLOSSARY:

as your uncle will frank it, it will cost William nothing: Sir Thomas, as a Member of Parliament, was entitled to frank a letter by signing it so that the recipient need not pay for it on delivery as was then usual

all the liberal dispositions of an eldest son: the eldest son usually inherited his father's house, land and money, to keep the estate intact; unlike Edmund, who will have to follow a profession, Tom feels he is well provided for, and can afford to be generous

Fanny could read, work, and write, but she had been taught nothing more: girls of good family did not usually go to school, but had a governess to teach them; the Prices were not rich enough to employ one. 'Work' is needle-work

put the map of Europe together: cut out countries and put them together again like a jigsaw puzzle (a way of learning geography)

Chapter 3

When Fanny is fifteen, Mr Norris dies, and Mrs Norris moves from the parsonage to the village; Sir Thomas expects that she will now have Fanny to live with her. This upsets Fanny, who tells Edmund; 'I love this house and every thing in it.' Mrs Norris, however, is too mean to have her. Sir Thomas and Lady Bertram, though surprised, are happy to keep Fanny with them. Dr Grant comes to live at the parsonage, taking Mr

Norris's place as rector (which should have been kept for Edmund by a temporary holder, but has had to be given up to pay for Tom's debts). After a year, Sir Thomas has to go to Antigua in the West Indies on business, and takes Tom with him to remove him from undesirable acquaintances.

NOTES AND GLOSSARY:

incumbent: holder of an ecclesiastical office

the expense of her support, and the obligation of her future provision: the expense of keeping her, and the responsibility of providing for her in the future. Sir Thomas is not so rich that he can easily take on the considerable expense of an extra dependent

the smallest habitation that could rank as genteel: the smallest house that was suitable for a person of good birth to live in. 'Gentility' is the desirable aim of behaving in a gentlemanly or gentlewomanly way

Sir Thomas's means will be rather straitened, if the Antigua estate is to make such poor returns: Sir Thomas will be short of money if he gets so little income from the estate

scarcely ever seen in her offices: Mrs Grant kept out of the cook's domain, that is, let her run everything herself

Chapter 4

Sir Thomas and Tom arrive safely in Antigua despite Mrs Norris's fears. Maria and Julia, accompanied to balls by Mrs Norris, are successfully established among the belles of the neighbourhood, while Fanny is content to stay at home with Lady Bertram.

When the old grey pony which she rides for exercise dies, Fanny finds that she must either stay in all day with the idle Lady Bertram or go for overstrenuous walks with the energetic Mrs Norris. To give her healthy exercise, Edmund exchanges a horse of his own for one suitable for her to ride. Fanny's feelings towards Edmund are 'respectful, grateful, confiding and tender'.

Tom returns, but Sir Thomas is delayed in the West Indies. Mrs Norris finds a husband for Maria, now twenty: Mr Rushworth, a rich but not very bright young man who has recently inherited one of the neighbourhood's finest houses and its large estate. They become engaged, and are to be married on Sir Thomas's return. Edmund fears that Maria is attracted only by Mr Rushworth's wealth.

Henry and Mary Crawford, the half-brother and half-sister of Mrs Grant, come to stay with her: they are 'young people of fortune', he with a good estate in Norfolk, she with twenty thousand pounds.

NOTES AND GLOSSARY:

how well Edmund could supply his place: the domestic duties of the head of the house can be seen in this list of 'carving, talking to the steward, writing to the attorney, settling with the servants'. Most wives would however have taken more part in directing the household than did Lady Bertram

Lady Bertram did not go into public with her daughters: when girls entered society, it was customary for them to be accompanied everywhere by their mother, or by an older married woman, called a 'chaperone'. Lady Bertram hands over this responsibility to Mrs Norris

Fanny had no share in the festivities of the season: 'the season' was the period of the year in which most people held their balls and parties; Fanny does not take part in them because she has not yet 'come out', that is, formally entered adult society. She does so unofficially at her first ball, the small one in Chapter 12, and Sir Thomas gives a special 'coming-out ball' for her in Chapter 28

the same interest: the same group of people, the landed gentry

had air and countenance: was of good appearance and expression

'Heaven's *last* best gift': from *Paradise Lost*, Book V, line 19, by John Milton (1606–74)

Chapter 5

The Crawfords and the Bertrams become friends, Maria and Julia admiring Mary's lively dark beauty, and finding Mr Crawford at first plain, then more and more handsome, until Julia is 'ready to be fallen in love with' by him. Maria sees no harm in liking him, despite her engagement, and he pays attentions to her. Mary Crawford finds much in Tom Bertram's favour – the house, the estate and the title. Fanny too admires Miss Crawford's beauty but thinks Mr Crawford plain. Mary Crawford is puzzled about Fanny's position, asking if she is 'out' in society yet.

NOTES AND GLOSSARY:

the reversion of Mansfield Park: the right of succession to the estate

seats: country mansions with parks

Chapter 6

Mr Rushworth asks for advice about improving his estate, Sotherton Court. He plans to cut down the avenue of trees, which Fanny deplores to Edmund: she wishes she could see Sotherton before the improvements are carried out. Edmund says he would prefer to do his own improvements rather than employ a landscape designer as Maria suggests. As she listens, Miss Crawford begins to admire him and to judge him 'a well bred man'. The company decides on a visit to Sotherton Court, and Mrs Norris says that they will all go except Fanny who must stay at home with Lady Bertram.

NOTES AND GLOSSARY:

his grounds laid out by an improver: to improve one's estate was to make alterations to it that increased its value, here especially by re-planning the landscape on 'picturesque' principles. To use an improver was to employ a professional adviser rather than to design the alterations oneself

Mr Repton   Humphrey Repton, one of the most prominent landscape designers, and author of *Observations on the Theory and Practice of Landscape Gardening* (1803)

their acquaintance had begun in delapidations: they first met when Dr Grant moved into the parsonage and they discussed any damage or deterioration that had taken place during the Norrises' time there

Cowper: William Cowper (1731–1800); the line Fanny quotes comes from his poem *The Task*, Book I, *The Sofa*, lines 338–9

passed over: not promoted

***Rears* and *Vices*:**   a Rear Admiral is two degrees lower than an Admiral, a Vice Admiral one degree lower. Miss Crawford is punning, in spite of her disclaimer

Chapter 7

Edmund and Fanny both consider that Miss Crawford speaks improperly about her uncle and her brother; but as she plays her harp beautifully and likes an audience, Edmund listens to her playing every day and starts to fall in love with her. Fanny is hurt when Edmund offers Miss Crawford the mare that she usually rides. Though a beginner, Miss Crawford proves an excellent rider, and keeps the mare beyond her time; Fanny, waiting, watches the enjoyment of the whole party in which she has no part. They go off without her 'four fine mornings successively'. On the last evening Edmund returns to find Fanny on the sofa with a headache, having been forced to pick roses in the hot sun for Lady Bertram and to walk twice to Mrs Norris's house and back. He is vexed with these two demanding women, and with himself for leaving her with no choice of company and no mare to ride; he resolves that this must never happen again.

NOTES AND GLOSSARY:
a wonderful play of feature: a mobile, expressive face
very indecorous: decorum, the order of things as they should be, is of great importance throughout the novel

Chapter 8

The visit to Sotherton is organised. When Edmund discovers that Fanny is to be left at home, he volunteers to keep his mother company himself instead, as he knows that Fanny dearly wishes to see Sotherton. Lady Bertram agrees but Mrs Norris objects to any change in her plan. In the end Mrs Grant offers herself as companion to Lady Bertram so that Edmund can go.

When they set off, Mrs Grant offers Julia the 'place of honour' on the box beside Henry Crawford who is driving: Maria is cross, but her spirits rise as they approach Sotherton, which will be hers when she marries Mr Rushworth.

NOTES AND GLOSSARY:
barouche: four-wheeled carriage with collapsible half-head, for four passengers facing each other in twos, and a driver sitting on a 'box' in front
consequence: importance, position
Court-Leet and Court-Baron: the estate included not merely its own house and land, but the village, cottages, a church and so on, as described during the drive

Chapter 9

Mrs Rushworth shows them the large, handsome house: Mary Crawford is unheeding, Fanny attentive. She expects more grandeur in the private chapel, and thinks it a pity that the custom of having daily family prayers has ceased. Mary Crawford speaks scathingly of clergymen, and is aghast when Julia says that if Edmund were already a clergyman, he could marry Maria and Mr Rushworth there and then.

Moving out of doors to look at the plants and 'curious pheasants', the party divides, Edmund, Mary Crawford and Fanny walking together through the 'wilderness' or 'nice little wood', shady and more natural than the park. Miss Crawford finds Edmund's chosen profession neither important nor influential: 'A clergyman is nothing.' The three sit for a while on a bench, but Miss Crawford and Edmund soon walk on to 'measure' the wood.

NOTES AND GLOSSARY:

collation: a light meal, at an unusual time. The main dinner was to be at five o'clock

curricle: light two-wheeled carriage, usually drawn by two horses abreast

the window tax: a tax imposed from 1696 to 1851 which levied a substantial amount for each window in a house

'Blown by the night wind of Heaven': from *The Lay of the Last Minstrel* by Sir Walter Scott

in orders ... ordained ... take orders: to take orders is to enter the ministry of the church; to be ordained is to enter that ministry in an ordination service performed by a bishop, which Edmund attends in Chapter 29

the cloth: the clerical profession

supposing the preacher to have the sense to prefer Blair's to his own: if the preacher has the sense to use a book of sermons in five volumes by Hugh Blair (1718–1800)

the *manners* I speak of, might rather be called *conduct*: this sentence explains Edmund's philosophy – he is drawing a distinction between fine manners and moral behaviour

a ha-ha: a sunken wall or fence forming a boundary, usually bordering a park or garden, to allow uninterrupted views

Chapter 10

Fanny, left on the bench, is joined by Maria Bertram, Mr Rushworth and Henry Crawford. Maria and Henry Crawford wish to go through an iron gate into the park, the better to view the house and discuss improvements, but it is locked. Mr Rushworth goes back to the house to fetch the key. Maria and Mr Crawford speak suggestively about the locked gate, edge past it, and are soon out of sight. Fanny, shocked, is again left alone. Julia appears, hot and cross in pursuit; she too scrambles across the fence.

Mr Rushworth at last appears with the key and is 'evidently mortified and displeased' that the others have gone through: he sits down with Fanny and criticises Mr Crawford's looks. Fanny persuades him to follow the others, then, weary of waiting, she walks off to find Edmund and Miss Crawford who are in 'the very avenue which Fanny had been hoping the whole morning to reach'.

They return to the house for dinner, 'having been all walking after each other'. On the way home Mr Crawford asks Julia to accompany him on the box, which displeases Maria. She travels inside with Fanny and Mrs Norris, who is well pleased with a basket of cream cheese, pheasants' eggs and herbs she has been given by the housekeeper and the gardener.

NOTES AND GLOSSARY:

'I cannot get out, as the starling said': alludes to a caged starling in *A Sentimental Journey* (1768) by Laurence Sterne (1713–68)

Quarterly Reviews: numbers of the literary and political journal *The Quarterly Review*, first published in 1809

Chapter 11

Maria and Julia are not looking forward to the homecoming of Sir Thomas, expected in November. Maria especially finds it 'a gloomy prospect', as it will bring her wedding to Mr Rushworth. Mary Crawford, Edmund and Fanny discuss the desirability of Edmund's becoming a clergyman. Miss Crawford feels he has been influenced by the fact that there is a 'living' or parish for him; Fanny disagrees; Edmund thinks he may have been, but 'blamelessly'. When Miss Crawford joins the Misses Bertram in singing, Edmund, instead of going out of doors to look at the stars with Fanny as they had planned, is drawn towards the singers, and leaves Fanny sighing alone in the window embrasure.

NOTES AND GLOSSARY:

a competence: enough money to live on

Chapter 12

When Tom Bertram returns to Mansfield Park, Mary Crawford finds that she prefers Edmund. Mr Crawford goes to Norfolk for a fortnight. When he returns, life falls into its previous pattern, and only Fanny is alarmed at his behaviour towards Maria and Julia. She hints her fears to Edmund, but he, like everybody else, thinks that Julia is going to be his choice. At Fanny's first ball (a dance spontaneously arranged because they have a musician and five couples to dance), Tom Bertram regales her with news of a sick horse, and only dances with her to escape playing cards with Mrs Norris and Dr Grant.

NOTES AND GLOSSARY:

Sir Thomas complete: Tom will be called Sir Thomas Bertram when his father dies, and will be 'complete' with his inheritance, Mansfield Park

complying with the common forms: it was not correct for a couple to dance too many times consecutively, but it would

have been permissible for Mr Rushworth and
Maria, as an engaged couple, to disregard this
convention

Chapter 13

The Honourable John Yates, a fashionable and extravagant new friend
of Tom Bertram's, comes to stay at Mansfield Park after visiting other
friends at Ecclesford, where they had planned some private theatricals.
He talks incessantly of the play, *Lovers' Vows*, which has had to be
cancelled because of the death of a relative, and awakens the Bertrams'
'inclination to act'. Tom discovers that the billiard-room is ideal for a
theatre, and Sir Thomas's room for a green-room. Edmund objects that
their father's sense of decorum would never permit them to act, that
putting on a play would be taking unjustifiable liberties with his house.
Fanny is equally shocked but hopes they may not be able to find a play
to suit all their tastes. While Edmund protests that he will not act, Henry
Crawford brings the message that his sister will be happy to take any
part. This silences Edmund at last. Mrs Norris, seeing prospects of
'hurry, bustle and importance', decides to live at Mansfield Park in
order to be constantly at their service.

NOTES AND GLOSSARY:

a tolerable independence: quite a large independent income
so near the long paragraph ... which would have immortalized the whole
          party: so near to being written up in what we would
          call the 'gossip columns' of the newspapers (as
          Maria's elopement is reported in Chapter 46)
The play had been Lovers' Vows: an English adaptation (1798) by Mrs
          Inchbald of a German play, *Das Kind der Liebe*
          (*Child of Love*, 1791) by A. von Kotzebue
My Grandmother: a musical farce by Prince Hoare (1793)
the jointure: estate settled on a wife, to be enjoyed by her father
          after her husband's death
Shylock or Richard III ... Julius Caesar ... to be'd and not be be'd: all
          references to tragedies by William Shakespeare
          (1564–1616): *The Merchant of Venice*, *Richard III*,
          Julius Caesar, *Hamlet*
green-room: actors' dressing-room
my name was Norval: a character in the popular *Douglas, a Tragedy* by
          John Home (1756)

Chapter 14

The carpentry work on the theatre and the making of green baize curtains are begun before a play is selected, each one proposed being opposed by somebody. At last, Tom's suggestion of *Lovers' Vows*, the very play which had been rehearsed at Ecclesford, is welcomed by all. Maria Bertram wants to play the heroine, Agatha, with Henry Crawford playing her son, Frederick. Julia also wants to play Agatha, and is hurt when Henry Crawford says that she is unsuitable for such a tragic part; she sees him exchange glances with Maria, and feels she has been tricked. Tom, as director, decides in favour of Maria and wishes Julia to take the minor comic role of the Cottager's Wife, with Miss Crawford as Amelia, the second lead. Henry Crawford protests that Julia should play Amelia, but she exclaims that if she is not to be Agatha she does not want any part, and rushes out of the room. Fanny reads through the play and is shocked that it should even be considered for private theatricals.

NOTES AND GLOSSARY:

Heir at Law: a play by George Colman (1797)

the situation of one: Agatha's situation is that of an unmarried mother, who has been seduced by Baron Wildenhaim (played by Mr Yates) and left with a son Frederick (Henry Crawford), now grown up. One of the plots concerns the reunion of Agatha and the Baron

the language of the other: Amelia, the Baron's daughter (played by Mary Crawford) speaks very improperly to her tutor, the clergyman Anhalt, about love and marriage; she wishes to marry him rather than her father's candidate, the rich, foppish Count Cassel (played by Mr Rushworth). It is the impropriety of Amelia's lines that forces Edmund to take the part of Anhalt so that Mary Crawford will not have to speak them to a stranger (see Chapter 16)

Chapter 15

Miss Crawford agrees to play Amelia, and Mr Rushworth, after much hesitation, settles on Count Cassel. Mr Yates is to play Baron Wildenhaim, Maria–Agatha's erstwhile seducer. When Edmund hears of the choice of the play, he expresses his strong disapproval. Lady Bertram then tells Maria not to act anything improper as her father would not like it, but Maria sees nothing objectionable in the play. Mrs Norris contends that if they do not act, the expense of the preparations so far will have been wasted. Mary Crawford urges Edmund to play Anhalt the clergyman and resents his reply that 'the man who chooses the profession itself is, perhaps, one of the last who would wish to represent it on the stage.' Tom and all the others press Fanny to play the

Cottager's Wife, but she refuses, in agitation. Mrs Norris sharply attacks her as 'very ungrateful indeed, considering who and what she is'. Edmund is 'too angry to speak'; Fanny is almost in tears. Mary Crawford speaks kindly to her, thus restoring herself to Edmund's favour. Tom says they will have to ask an acquaintance, Charles Maddox, to play Anhalt.

NOTES AND GLOSSARY:

by no means what I expected: Mary Crawford here articulates what everyone feels – the importance of having the right performer 'opposite' one in the play.

Chapter 16

Upset by Tom's pressure and her aunt's attack, Fanny seeks refuge in the East room, which holds all her small possessions, and comforts her, though Mrs Norris has 'stipulated for there never being a fire in it on Fanny's account'. She wonders if she is right to refuse to act: or is she being selfish? Edmund comes into ask her advice upon his own dilemma: if the others ask Charles Maddox to play Anhalt, the resultant over-familiarity with a mere acquaintance will be 'the end of all the privacy and propriety which was talked about at first', and playing Amelia to a stranger will be objectionable to Mary Crawford. Should he therefore take the part himself? Fanny is sorry to see Edmund drawn into doing what he had decided against – a triumph, she feels, for the others – but he goes away thinking he has won her approval.

NOTES AND GLOSSARY:

transparencies: pictures painted on canvas or muslin to be shown up by light behind them when placed in a window

Lord Macartney: George, Lord Macartney (1737–1806), British Ambassador to China, whose *Plates to his Embassy to China* and *Journal of the Embassy* were published in 1796 and 1807

Crabbe's Tales: George Crabbe's (1754–1832) *Tales* in verse, published in 1812

the Idler: *The Idler* was a series of contributions by Samuel Johnson to the *Universal Chronicle or Weekly Gazette,* from 1758 to 1760

Chapter 17

Tom Bertram and Maria are delighted with their 'victory over Edmund's discretion' while Mary Crawford's renewed cheerfulness makes Edmund feel he has made the right decision. Mrs Grant takes on the part of the Cottager's Wife, leaving Fanny relieved, but isolated from the others' activity. Henry Crawford pays attentions to Maria (who never considers Mr Rushworth), and ignores Julia, who either sits alone in gloomy silence or ridicules the acting of the others to Mr Yates. She still loves Henry Crawford, and feels her sister to be 'her greatest enemy'.

NOTES AND GLOSSARY:

might represent the county: might be a Member of Parliament

Hawkins Browne's 'Address to Tobacco': Isaac Hawkins Browne (1705–60) wrote a pastiche poem called 'A Pipe of Tobacco: in Imitation of Six Several Authors'

Chapter 18

Edmund is annoyed because Tom has employed an expensive scene painter. Fanny, 'being always a very courteous listener', hears everybody's parts, and listens to their complaints; she begins to enjoy watching the acting, particularly that of Mr Crawford, of whom Mr Rushworth is now very jealous. Lady Bertram asks what the play is about, and is told she will see it rehearsed next day. To escape yet another 'most unnecessary rehearsal' between Henry Crawford and Maria, Fanny retreats to the East room, where first Mary Crawford and then Edmund come to ask her to hear their parts. Delighted, they rehearse together, to Fanny's agitation.

The first full rehearsal of the first three acts is set back by the news that Mrs Grant cannot come. Everyone, even Edmund, asks Fanny to play her part. She wavers. The others begin, making too much noise to hear any other sounds in the house: the door is thrown open and Julia appears, exclaiming 'My father is come! He is in the hall at this moment.'

Chapter 19

Sir Thomas's arrival causes consternation. He greets his family and receives Fanny affectionately. His manner seems changed; his frightening dignity seems 'lost in tenderness'. He is the life of the party, the centre of his family, the leader of the conversation. Lady Bertram, delighted at his early return, moves her dog Pug, and gives 'all her attention and all the rest of her sofa to her husband'. He meets Mr Rushworth and finds nothing disagreeable in his appearance, Mrs Norris having whisked away his pink satin cloak. But Sir Thomas soon discovers candles in his room, 'confusion in the furniture' and Mr Yates noisily rehearsing in his ranting style. Mr Yates blunders on about the theatricals, not sensing Sir Thomas's disapproval.

NOTES AND GLOSSARY:
I have hardly taken a gun out since the 3rd: Tom is deflecting the
conversation from theatricals to shooting, a major
part of the sporting life of an English gentleman.
The pheasants were bred on the estate, and a well-
stocked estate was essential – hence Tom's assurance
that they had not shot too many

Chapter 20

The next morning Edmund goes to see his father, tries to explain his
reasons for agreeing to the theatricals and is careful to say nothing
unkind about the others while stressing that Fanny only is blameless. Sir
Thomas determines to 'lose the disagreeable impression' when the house
is cleared of all reminders of the theatricals, and 'restored to its proper
state', but he feels it necessary to express his disapproval of Mrs Norris's
acquiescence in the play. Mr Yates is disappointed that there are to be no
more rehearsals or performances.

Maria hopes for a declaration from Mr Crawford, but he leaves for
Bath; although he professes regret, she knows his engagements are
fabrications. Her spite supports her, but she suffers severe agony of
mind. Julia rejoices for selfish reasons, Fanny for purer ones. Mr Yates,
equally offensive to Sir Thomas as Tom's friend and as Julia's admirer
finally leaves. Mrs Norris takes the stage curtain off to her cottage
'where she happened to be particularly in want of green baize'.

NOTES AND GLOSSARY:
to see his steward and his bailiff: to see the people in charge of his lands
and his tenants. Sir Thomas's responsibilities
include control of 'business . . . stables . . . gardens
. . . plantations', as well as the domestic duties
mentioned in Chapter 4
It is early for Bath. – You will find nobody there: The 'season' for going to
Bath, a fashionable spa in the south-west of
England, was later in the winter – this is late
October or early November

Chapter 21

Sir Thomas prefers to be alone with his own family, and draws back
from intimacy with the Grant houshold, which Edmunds regrets: Fanny
alone is entertained by her uncle's talk about the West Indies. Edmund
tells her that Sir Thomas admires her improved looks.

Sir Thomas concludes that Mr Rushworth is 'an inferior young man',
and that Maria is indifferent to him. He asks her if she wishes to break

off the engagement, but she says she does not. Having heard nothing from Henry Crawford, she is now determined from 'pride and self-revenge' to marry Mr Rushworth. She wants to enjoy the independence she has tasted during her father's absence, and to escape the restrictions of Mansfield Park. Mrs Rushworth goes to live in Bath, leaving Sotherton to its new mistress, Maria, and 'a very proper wedding' takes place, to Mrs Norris's self-congratulation. The couple plans to take a house in Brighton, then to go to London. Julia accompanies them – since their rivalry has ceased, the sisters have recovered their 'former good understanding'.

NOTES AND GLOSSARY:

chariot: a closed four-wheeled carriage with the two passengers facing the horses

Julia was to go with them: it was usual for a close female relative to accompany the bride on her honeymoon

Chapter 22

Fanny, as the only young woman left at home, has a more important position than before. A visit to the parsonage (to shelter from a rainstorm) starts an uncertain new intimacy with Miss Crawford, who reflects with surprise that she has been five months at Mansfield. She finds herself unexpectedly reconciled to the notion of spending half the year in the country in a moderately sized residence (such as Edmund could have as a clergyman), though she sees problems in living in the country. Edmund is pleased that she and Fanny are friends. Mrs Grant unexpectedly invites Fanny with Edmund to dine at the parsonage.

NOTES AND GLOSSARY:

the only young woman in the drawing-room: the drawing-room was the special place of the ladies of the house, who 'withdrew' there after dinner. The gentlemen joined them later, after drinking port and smoking

your eldest cousin is gone so that he _may_ be Mr Bertram again: see note to Chapter 1. When the eldest son, known as 'Mr Bertram' is away, the next eldest left at home becomes the 'senior' son and is called 'Mr Bertram' instead of 'Mr Edmund Bertram'. Its 'younger-brother-like' sound has unpleasant connotations for Miss Crawford as the elder brother will inherit the title and estate. 'Mr Edmund' is very insignificant compared with _Lord_ Edmund or _Sir_ Edmund – she does not care as Fanny does for the name itself, only for the title. See her letter to Fanny in Chapter 45

Chapter 23

Lady Bertram is surprised that Fanny has been invited by the Grants, her first invitation to dine out. On their way to the parsonage, Edmund praises her appearance. To their surprise, Henry Crawford has just arrived there. He speaks of 'Rushworth and his fair bride', 'with a significant smile which made Fanny quite hate him'.

Dr Grant and Edmund discuss the 'living' or parish Edmund will have when he becomes a clergyman in a few weeks' time. Mary Crawford is mortified that Edmund is to take orders, despite her objections. She resolves to match him in indifference.

NOTES AND GLOSSARY:

cadet: younger son

Chapter 24

Henry Crawford tells Mary that he intends to amuse himself for a fortnight by making Fanny fall in love with him. 'She is now absolutely pretty'; he has never met a girl like her. His sister asks him not to make Fanny 'really unhappy'.

Fanny's defence against Henry Crawford is that her affections are 'engaged elsewhere' (with Edmund), so that he cannot harm her peace of mind, though she dislikes him less than formerly. William writes to say that he is back in England, his ship, the *Antwerp*, lying at anchor at Spithead. Sir Thomas invites William to stay at Mansfield Park; when he arrives he is well received, and his uncle encourages him to talk of his adventures at sea.

Chapter 25

The families from Mansfield Park and the parsonage renew their intimacy, encouraged now by Sir Thomas, who notices that Henry Crawford admires Fanny. After dinner at the parsonage, they play cards. Henry Crawford teaches Lady Bertram and Fanny to play, urging Fanny to play to win. Mary Crawford makes enormous bids, and wins, though without winning back what she has paid.

Henry Crawford tells Edmund that he has seen the parsonage of his prospective parish, Thornton Lacey, and is full of ideas for its improvement, which Edmund resists. Henry Crawford offers to rent it from him, but Edmund wants to live in it himself – he and Sir Thomas believe a clergyman should live in his parish to help his parishioners, not merely preach there once a week. This dispels Mary Crawford's dream of Edmund living in a fine house.

NOTES AND GLOSSARY:

after making up the Whist table: after gathering together the four persons necessary to play whist, a card game played in sequences of three games, called 'rubbers', between the same pairs

Speculation: a round game of cards in which the players buy and sell trump cards, the holder of the highest trump card in a round winning the pool

private secretary to the first Lord: (of the Admiralty), that is, able to exert influence to secure William's promotion

the Assembly night: the night of an important ball

has not a commission: is not an officer

Chapter 26

To fulfil William's wish to see Fanny dance, Sir Thomas decides to hold a ball at Mansfield Park (despite Mrs Norris's objection that Maria and Julia are away). Fanny worries about what to wear; she has one pretty ornament, an amber cross given to her by William, but no chain to wear it on. Edmund is preoccupied with his ordination as a clergyman which is due to take place that week, and with his prospects of marrying Mary Crawford. Does she love him enough to do without London life and society?

Miss Crawford asks Fanny to choose a necklace from her jewel box to wear with the amber cross and to keep. Fanny is confused but chooses the necklace she thinks Miss Crawford wishes her to have, though it is less plain than she herself would have liked. She is disturbed when Miss Crawford says it was originally a gift to her from Henry. She overrides Fanny's protests about accepting it.

NOTES AND GLOSSARY:

She should have to do the honours of the evening: she would have to act as hostess, rendering civilities to the guests

coze: chat

Chapter 27

When Fanny returns to the East room, she finds Edmund there, writing a note to her to accompany a simple gold chain, just such a one as she had wished for. Touched and grateful, she asks what to do about Miss Crawford's necklace; he says it would be unkind to return it: he wants there to be no shadow of coolness between the 'two dearest objects I have on earth'. These words tell Fanny that he intends to marry Miss Crawford, who she thinks does not deserve him. She is thrown into confusion and dejection.

Mr Crawford offers to take William back to Portsmouth in his carriage, to dine with his uncle the Admiral, after the ball. Fanny does not realise that this is to be her 'coming out ball', her first true public appearance. Dispirited by a day spent with the angry Mrs Norris, she meets Edmund, who has been to the parsonage to ask Miss Crawford for the first two dances. She has agreed, but has said that this will be their last dance together – 'she never has danced with a clergyman, she says, and she never will.' Full of joy that he should confide his grief in her, Fanny dresses for the ball, and is pleased with her own looks. The necklace will not go through the ring of the cross, so she wears the chain with it, and the necklace separately.

NOTES AND GLOSSARY:

travelling post: to travel in one's own carriage, hiring fresh horses at each stage. William feels as if he were 'going up with dispatches', that is, taking urgent messages to Naval Headquarters in London, instead of going up 'by the mail', that is, by public mail-coach

Chapter 28

Fanny's dress and her beauty please Sir Thomas. She is happy when Edmund asks her for two dances. When Mr Crawford asks her for the first two dances, she is glad to have a partner but disturbed by his glance at the necklace. To her dismay she discovers that she must 'open the ball', that is, lead the first dance. She does so well and gracefully, to Sir Thomas's pleasure. Mary Crawford tells her that Henry is only going to London for William's sake. She dances 'in sober tranquillity' with Edmund, pleased to be his friend; he and Miss Crawford have parted 'with mutual vexation'. At three o'clock Thomas sends Fanny to bed, giving her permission to breakfast with William before his early departure. Sir Thomas is to join them, and disappoints Fanny by inviting Mr Crawford as well.

NOTES AND GLOSSARY:

her progress down the dance: the dancers stood in two facing lines in a 'set', and between them danced the first couple, from one end to the other (in this way Fanny does 'rather walk than dance down the shortening set', when she is tired, and there are fewer and fewer dancers)

securing her at that part of the evening: one spent the supper-hour with one's partner for the dance immediately preceding it; Henry Crawford wishes for the extended time to talk to Fanny

the Lady of Branxholm Hall: in *The Lay of the Last Minstrel* (I,20), by
Sir Walter Scott
negus: hot, sweetened wine and water

Chapter 29

Edmund goes to Peterborough to stay with a friend, Mr Owen, who is
also to be ordained. Fanny tries to talk to Lady Bertram, who cannot
remember anything about the ball. Mary Crawford finds Edmund's
absence painful, and regrets speaking so sharply to him at the ball.
When he stays on at Peterborough with Mr Owen (who has sisters), she
feels 'one disagreeable emotion entirely new to her – jealousy'. In
desperation she questions Fanny, who replies calmly that she knows
'nothing of the Miss Owens'. Does she expect a marriage? Fanny says
no; nor does she think that Edmund is likely to 'marry at all – or not at
present'.

NOTES AND GLOSSARY:
cribbage . . . four in hand and eight in crib: cribbage is a card game for two,
three or four persons

Chapter 30

Henry Crawford returns from London with a surprise for his sister – he
is 'quite determined to marry Fanny Price'. Mary is astonished, but 'not
displeased with her brother's marrying a little beneath him'. Mary tells
him that Fanny will never marry without love, 'but ask her to love you,
and she will never have the heart to refuse'. He praises Fanny's beauty of
face, figure and disposition. He plans to let his own house and settle in
Northamptonshire; Mary can stay half the year with them. She is
delighted to see him 'so much in love' – what will Julia and Maria think?
He replies that they will be angry, but that everyone will behave
differently to Fanny now because of him.

NOTES AND GLOSSARY:
'the pleasing plague': love, thus alluded to in William Whitehead's 'The
Je ne scai Quoi, a song', published in *Dodsley's
Collection of Poems by Several Hands*, 1801

Chapter 31

Henry Crawford tells Fanny that through his uncle he has secured
William's promotion to lieutenant. She is distressed when he tells her
that everything he has done for William is 'to be placed to the account of
his excessive and unequalled attachment to her', and offers 'himself,

hand, fortune, every thing to her acceptance'. He presses her for an answer; she is confused and will not listen, rushing away when Sir Thomas enters, to walk agitatedly up and down in the East room.

She is vexed to find that Sir Thomas has invited Henry to dine that day. At dinner he gives her a note from his sister encouraging her to accept him – 'Go on, my dear Fanny, and without fear.' Fanny is silent throughout dinner, 'earnestly trying to understand what Mr and Miss Crawford were at'. Henry Crawford insists that she reply to his sister, and she writes a confused letter begging her never to mention the subject again.

Chapter 32

Next morning, Fanny is amazed to see Mr Crawford arrive early again. Sir Thomas comes up to her in the East room, and is surprised to find that there is no fire despite the snowy weather. Mr Crawford has come to ask for Fanny's hand in marriage. Sir Thomas is astonished to find that she means to refuse him, and considers her unreasonable, in view of Mr Crawford's 'situation in life, fortune, and character'. She cannot mention Henry Crawford's lack of principle without implicating Maria and Julia. Sir Thomas tells her sternly that she is wilful and perverse. Fanny declares that she could never make Mr Crawford happy, and would herself be miserable. She is reluctant to speak to Mr Crawford and Sir Thomas goes down to do so on her behalf, leaving Fanny wretched. When he returns, he tells her that Mr Crawford is no longer pressing to see her, advises her to take a walk in the shrubbery to recover from her tears, and undertakes not to tell her aunts of the proposal.

Returning from her walk, Fanny finds a fire burning in her room on Sir Thomas's instructions; it is to be lit for her every day. After dinner, she is told that Sir Thomas wishes to speak to her in his room; she finds herself alone with Mr Crawford.

NOTES AND GLOSSARY:
on the gravel: on the gravelled walks of the shrubbery

Chapter 33

Henry Crawford is inclined to think that Fanny loves him, 'though she might not know it herself'. He himself is very much in love, and determined to make her love him, not knowing that she has 'a pre-engaged heart'. Fanny now sees him as a more upright man than the one who trifled with Maria at Sotherton but she becomes angry that he will not accept her refusal.

Sir Thomas is impressed by Henry Crawford's perseverance. He has to tell Lady Bertram and Mrs Norris of the proposal as it is being freely discussed at the parsonage. Mrs Norris is furious that Mr Crawford should have proposed to Fanny rather than to Julia. Lady Bertram is pleased that Fanny has been 'sought in marriage by a man of fortune' and takes it as proof of her beauty.

Chapter 34

Having extended his visit to avoid Miss Crawford, Edmund is surprised to find her and her brother still at the parsonage on his return. She greets him warmly, with no shadow of their previous disagreement. Sir Thomas tells him of Henry Crawford's proposal to Fanny, and he feels that Crawford has spoken too early, but may yet persuade Fanny to accept him.

When Henry Crawford reads Shakespeare aloud, Fanny is drawn by his magnificent reading. Even Lady Bertram praises him, and supposes that he will have a theatre at his house at Everingham when he is settled there. He says 'Oh! no', with an expressive smile at Fanny. Edmund considers that the clergy should cultivate the art of reading. Henry Crawford asks him many questions about the church. He would like to be a fine preacher – but he must have a London parish, and only preach now and then, 'not for a constancy'. While Edmund reads a newspaper to allow them to talk alone, Henry Crawford entangles Fanny in explanations about his use of the word 'constancy'. He declares that he is unequal to her in goodness but 'it is not by equality of merit' that she will be won; the man who sees and loves her goodness will win her.

Chapter 35

At Sir Thomas's suggestion Edmund talks to Fanny; he tells her that Crawford's proposal is 'advantageous and desirable', but only if she can return his affection, which comforts her, until he continues that she must let Crawford win her over. They have 'moral and literary tastes in common', and other qualities that are complementary. She can never forget how improperly he behaved to Maria, how unfeelingly to Mr Rushworth. Edmund says they *all* behaved badly. She will be good for Henry Crawford, and will 'make him everything' – a responsibility she does not want.

Edmund is impressed by Miss Crawford's approval of the match though it is not an advantageous one from the worldly point of view. He thinks the explanation of Fanny's refusal is her dislike of change.

Chapter 36

Edmund tells his father that Fanny may well return Henry Crawford's affection, given time, but Sir Thomas fears she may take too much time. Mary Crawford visits Fanny in her East room and recalls her rehearsal there with Edmund. She wishes she were not going to London, or that Fanny were coming with her so that she might understand the magnitude of her conquest of Henry Crawford by seeing other women's jealousy. Surely Fanny was not unprepared – what about his devotion at the ball – 'and . . . before the ball, the necklace!' Fanny is upset that the gift was really from him, but his gallantries often mean nothing. The Crawfords leave for London the following day.

NOTES AND GLOSSARY:

the two long speeches: Anhalt's speeches describing the good marriage and the unhappy marriage

Chapter 37

Sir Thomas hopes that Fanny will miss Henry Crawford, but cannot see signs of this: nor can Edmund think she misses his sister. Fanny has many fears about Miss Crawford, who now seems likely to marry Edmund. She may love him but she does not deserve him.

William arrives on ten days' leave. Sir Thomas decides that it would be good for Fanny to go back with him to Portsmouth to visit her family: she is more likely to appreciate what Mr Crawford has offered her when she is in the comparative poverty of her family's house. Fanny looks forward to being at home again, 'with her equals, whom she loves and and who love her'. Edmund promises to write to her when he has 'anything worth writing about' (the glow in his face tells her he means an engagement to Miss Crawford). She and William leave before breakfast.

NOTES AND GLOSSARY:

as already advanced one stage: as having already changed horses once at a staging post

Chapter 38

Fanny and William arrive at their parents' house in Portsmouth, after two days' journey. A 'trollopy-looking maidservant' meets them with the news that William's ship, the *Thrush*, has gone out of harbour, and that Mr Campbell, a brother officer, hopes William will go to her with him at six o'clock. Fanny is welcomed by her mother and by her two sisters, Susan, 'a well-grown fine girl of fourteen', and Betsey, the youngest of the family, about five. She is taken to a tiny parlour. Her mother is too preoccupied with William and the *Thrush* to pay any attention to Fanny. She has not prepared a meal, and even tea proves difficult to arrange: eventually Susan brings it. The fire is low, the house full of noise and bustle. Fanny's father greets her briefly and seems 'very much inclined to forget her again'. Two more brothers, Tom and Charles, rosy-faced, 'ragged and dirty, about eight and nine years old', appear; like the rest of the family, they make a dreadful noise, which almost stuns Fanny. She finds herself alone with her father, who reads a borrowed newspaper by the light of the only candle. Fanny feels very unimportant to her family; they ask nothing about herself or Mansfield Park.

Mr Campbell takes William off to the *Thrush*. Fanny is shocked to find Susan and Betsey fighting over a knife that another sister, Mary, had left Susan on her deathbed. Fatigued, she goes to bed in the cramped room which she is to share with Susan, thinking 'with respect' of her own little room at Mansfield Park.

NOTES AND GLOSSARY:

prize money: share in booty taken from ships they have successfully attacked

Chapter 39

Fanny is sadly disappointed with her family's disorderly house. Even worse, she cannot respect her parents, finding her father coarse, her mother slatternly. She tries to be useful, helping to prepare clothes for Sam, who is going as a cabin-boy aboard William's ship. She despairs of being able to love or help the younger boys or the spoilt Betsey, and she has many doubts about Susan's temper. In the incessant noise, she misses the elegance, harmony and peace of Mansfield Park.

NOTES AND GLOSSARY:

navy-list: official publication containing a list of the officers of the Navy, and other nautical information
her foreign education: her alien upbringing
Dr Johnson's celebrated judgment: 'Marriage has many pains, but celibacy has no pleasures' (from *Rasselas* (1759), Chapter 26, by Samuel Johnson)

Chapter 40

Fanny receives a rare letter from Mary Crawford, full of gossip. Maria and Julia are in London, the former enraged by any mention of Fanny. Mr Yates continues to be devoted to Julia. Edmund has not yet come to London. Fanny welcomes news of this society, as she finds no satisfaction in that of Portsmouth. Her one consolation is that Susan shows more promise than she had expected: her faults are caused by her perception that much is wrong at home. Fanny grows to admire her for trying to improve matters by herself. She tries to guide her away from the excesses of her methods, and buys Betsey a knife to stop the squabbling over the one bequeathed by Mary. Fanny and Susan sit together working and reading upstairs in the mornings, out of the noise. Fanny dreads the letter from Edmund that will tell her that he has spoken to Miss Crawford.

NOTES AND GLOSSARY:

A poor honourable is no catch: Mr Yates, as the younger son of a Lord has no title except the form 'the Honourable John Yates'; he is therefore no very advantageous match

circulating library: books were expensive, and there were no free public libraries; one could subscribe to a 'circulating library' which furnished books and literary journals to its members

Chapter 41

To Fanny's astonishment, Henry Crawford comes to visit her. Mrs Price's manners are at their best as she thanks him for his kindness to William. He tells Fanny that Edmund is in London and she feels that by now all must be settled between him and Miss Crawford. Henry Crawford takes Fanny and Susan out for a walk; they meet Mr Price, who is less objectionable than usual, and takes them to see the dockyard. Henry Crawford is full of information and amusing conversation. He discusses his estate at Everingham, his agent and tenants, and some business, talks of Mansfield Park, and tells Fanny that he has come to Portsmouth only to see her. To her relief he declines to join them for dinner, but promises to see them the following day.

Chapter 42

Mr Crawford accompanies the Prices to church, and for a walk on the ramparts: they look their best in their Sunday clothes. It is a beautiful day. Fanny is grateful for Mr Crawford's arm; he is convinced that she is not well, that the house is not healthy for her. She has been at Portsmouth for a month and is expecting to stay one more month. Henry Crawford tells her that if she ever wishes to go back earlier, he and his sister will take her back to Mansfield Park. He plans to go back to Everingham to deal with his tenants and agent.

Fanny returns home, with little heart for the ill-prepared food and ill-washed dishes. She feels deserted, and very low. She fancies she has seen a 'wonderful improvement in Mr Crawford', not taking account of the contrast with her present circle.

Chapter 43

Fanny receives a letter from Mary Crawford, telling her that Edmund is in London. Henry cannot be spared to attend to his estate as she wants him for a party at which he will see the Rushworths. Fanny speculates about Miss Crawford's true feelings for Edmund, and concludes that she will accept him in the end, despite the attractions of London.

Fanny continues to teach Susan, and read with her, and talk 'not always on subjects so high as history or morals', but also about Mansfield Park. Susan, who has 'an innate taste for the genteel and well-appointed', longs to go there, and Fanny realises that Susan is 'very little better fitted for home than her elder sister'; indeed, it would be a blessing if she had a home to invite her to. If she could only return Mr Crawford's regard, he would probably agree to such a plan 'most pleasantly'.

NOTES AND GLOSSARY:

luckily there is no distinction of dress now-a-days: clergyman did not wear special distinguishing clothes such as black suits or clerical collars at the time: Mary Crawford would not have wished Edmund's profession to be known

Saint George's, Hanover-Square: the most fashionable London church for weddings

Chapter 44

Fanny at last receives the long-expected letter from Edmund. His hopes of Miss Crawford are 'much weaker'; the fashionable world is his rival, rather than any one person. Henry Crawford and Maria have not met as friends, and Edmund regrets 'that Mrs Rushworth would resent any former supposed slight to Miss Bertram'. Julia 'seems to enjoy London exceedingly'. Sir Thomas cannot fetch Fanny until after Easter.

A letter from Lady Bertram informs Fanny that Tom is dangerously ill: 'a neglected fall, and a good deal of drinking' have brought on a fever, and Edmund is to bring him back to Mansfield Park. A second letter tells Fanny that Tom is near death.

Chapter 45

Lady Bertram is reassured by an apparent improvement in Tom's condition, but Edmund writes to Fanny that he is still in great danger. Easter comes, but still Sir Thomas cannot come for Fanny: she realises that Mansfield Park, not Portsmouth, is now her home. Lady Bertram misses her, all the more so as neither Maria nor Julia has gone home to comfort her. Mary Crawford, after a long interval, writes a letter which shocks Fanny. It anticipates Tom's death, which would bring the baronetcy and the estate to Edmund, in which event she would overlook his being a clergyman. Henry Crawford has just arrived, having seen Maria Rushworth in Richmond. Fanny is disgusted at what Miss Crawford says about Tom, and shocked that Henry Crawford is still 'the acquaintance, the flirt, perhaps, of Mrs Rushworth'.

NOTES AND GLOSSARY:

hectic symptoms: signs of the fever that accompanies a decline (any disease in which the sufferer wastes away to death; usually, as here, consumption (tuberculosis))

Cowper's Tirocinium: a poem by William Cowper, 'Tirocinium: or, A Review of Schools' (1785) in which he attacks public schools. The relevant line (1.562) is part of a description of a boy at school counting the days until he can go home

Chapter 46

Fanny receives another disturbing letter from Mary Crawford, warning her not to believe a 'most scandalous, ill-natured rumour' that may reach her. Her father reads a newspaper report of 'a matrimonial *fracas* in the family of Mr R. of Wimpole Street': 'the beautiful Mrs R. . . . having quitted her husband's roof in company with the well known and captivating Mr C.' Fanny knows the report is confirmed by Miss Crawford's letter. The whole family will suffer, particularly Edmund. A letter arrives from him with the news that Henry Crawford and Maria cannot be traced, and, moreover, that Julia has eloped to Scotland with Mr Yates. Sir Thomas wishes Fanny to return to Mansfield Park for Lady Bertram's sake, and he invites Susan to go with her for a few months. Edmund will come to Portsmouth to collect them next day. He arrives, looking very upset and ill. The return journey is sad and silent. On their arrival Lady Bertram comes forward to meet them with 'Dear Fanny! now I shall be comfortable.'

Chapter 47

Everybody at Mansfield Park has been miserable, especially Mrs Norris, who is stupefied by the failure of the marriage she prided herself on. Susan is happy, in spite of being left to herself because of everyone's worries. Lady Bertram finds relief in telling Fanny the details: Maria had gone to Twickenham, to stay with friends who were also close friends of Henry Crawford. Mr Rushworth's mother is bitter and hostile. Julia's elopement is 'a bad thing, done in the worst manner, and at the worst time'.

After a long time, Edmund talks to Fanny. He has seen Mary Crawford and been distressed to find that she sees mere indiscretion in the behaviour of her brother and Maria; she feels no 'modest loathing' of what they have done, and only blames them for being found out. She has made light of Edmund's distress, asking him if his serious words are 'part of his last sermon'. During their conversation Fanny is able to reassure Edmund that she feels no pain about Henry Crawford.

Chapter 48

Fanny, despite all the misery, is happy in Sir Thomas's renewed approval, in her usefulness, and in knowing that Edmund is no longer the dupe of Miss Crawford. Sir Thomas blames himself for letting selfish and worldly considerations stop him from preventing Maria's marriage. Julia's match is not too disastrous, Mr Yates being richer and more amenable than they had thought. Tom is restored to health, and becomes steady and quiet. Sir Thomas realises that Maria and Julia have suffered from being treated with indulgence and flattery by Mrs Norris, and with severity by himself. They have been educated for 'elegance and accomplishments', not for high moral principles, self-denial or humility.

Maria and Mr Crawford do not marry: she lives with him in hopes of marriage until they part enemies. Mr Rushworth divorces her. She has 'destroyed her . . . character' too irrecoverably to be received in her father's house or social circle, and eventually she and Mrs Norris go away to live together, their tempers becoming 'their mutual punishment'. Henry Crawford has lost Fanny, the one woman whom he has 'rationally, as well as passionately loved'. The Grants move to London, and Mrs Grant, soon widowed, sets up house with Mary Crawford, who is 'long in finding . . . any one' who can satisfy the better taste she has acquired at Mansfield. She finds it hard to put Edmund out of her mind. He has no such difficulty: scarcely has he stopped regretting Mary Crawford than he finds Fanny has grown very dear to him. Sir Thomas approves their marriage. William's continued good conduct and rising fame please him too. Susan takes Fanny's place as Lady Bertram's companion.

After their marriage, Fanny and Edmund live for a time at Thornton Lacey, until he receives the Mansfield living on the death of Dr Grant, and they move to the parsonage there; their happiness 'must appear as secure as earthly happiness can be', and the parsonage is perfect in Fanny's eyes, 'as every thing else, within the view and the patronage of Mansfield Park, has long been'.

NOTES AND GLOSSARY:

succeeded to a stall in Westminster: became a Canon of Westminster Cathedral

Part 3

Commentary

Subject and scope

Mansfield Park is about the necessity of finding and being true to one's own individuality, and of preserving society's established order and traditions. The individual must fit into society: not by submerging or denying his true self, but by accepting and developing it. This is not merely a matter of not offending against society (as Henry Crawford does by trifling with Julia and eloping with the newly married Maria); one must not isolate oneself from it, as Fanny is in danger of doing. When we first meet her, she has neither found herself nor succeeded in integrating herself into the society in which she finds herself. She yearns, yet fears, to be 'of consequence to any body'. She has failed to become other than the child-outsider who first arrived at Mansfield Park – Sir Thomas rightly fears that William 'must find his sister at sixteen in some respects too much like his sister at ten'.

It is not until Fanny separates herself mentally from her own family in Portsmouth that she becomes her adult, responsible, comforting, strong-minded self, and that she admits to herself that Mansfield Park is her true home. We realise that her romantic idea of Portsmouth as her home has no foundation in real life; when she does visit her family, Fanny is the stranger that she has been for eight years; her 'foreign education' at Mansfield has already separated her from her parents, and so have her own intellect, her innate good taste, and Edmund's guidance. (It is made clear that Fanny is not unique: Susan is by nature out of sympathy with the disorderly Price household, from which she separates herself without Fanny's pain and reluctance.) Fanny's development from childish awkwardness and isolation as she moves into the adult world involves facing many realities, both socially and mentally. She must 'come out' into society, and dance at a ball, and be introduced to people and 'do the honours' (Chapter 28). She must learn to act as confessor and mentor to her mentor, Edmund (Chapters 27, 47–8); she must follow her own instinct to teach (Susan, Chapters 40, 43), and comfort (Lady Bertram and Edmund, Chapters 47–8), and above all to have faith in her own judgment, confirmed by the baseness of Henry and Mary Crawford (Chapters 46–8).

Social setting

Houses and estates

The crucial influence on Fanny is Mansfield Park itself. Without obtrusively calling our attention to details, Jane Austen gives us a very clear picture of a beautiful, smoothly running house and estate. Mansfield Park is the product of riches well-guarded and well-spent, of generations of Sir Thomases planning, managing, conserving and 'improving' house and estate. All Sir Thomas's efforts go to achieving a harmonious, comfortable and elegant way of life. One of the ways by which we understand the harmony of Mansfield Park is by contrast with the dreadful Price household (Chapters 38–46): words such as 'poky', 'tiny', 'cramped' are opposed to its 'spaciousness' and 'grandeur'. The Price house is 'the abode of noise, disorder, and impropriety. Nobody was in their right place, nothing was done as it ought to be,' whereas 'at Mansfield, no sounds of contention, no raised voice, no abrupt bursts, no tread of violence was ever heard; all proceeded in a regular course of cheerful orderliness; every body had their due importance; every body's feelings were consulted.' There is certainly a connection between wealth and order: one cannot run a Mansfield Park on no money. But wealth is not all: a house takes its character from its master or mistress.

As well as Mansfield Park, we are shown another fine house, Sotherton (Chapters 8–10), in fuller detail, probably because Fanny is more experienced and observant than when she arrived at Mansfield Park. It is Elizabethan, 'a large, regular brick building – heavy, but respectable-looking'. We see 'rooms, all lofty, and many large, and amply furnished in the taste of fifty years back, with shining floors, solid mahogany, rich damask, marble, gilding and carving', and especially its mahogany chapel, so lacking in gothic-romantic appurtenances – 'no aisles, no arches, no inscriptions, no banners'. As we drive up to it, we are also aware of all that goes with such a house: its own village, cottages, church, alms-houses, steward's house, avenue of oaks. Above all, we become familiar with its park, and the many different kinds of landscape embraced by it: the wilderness, or regularly planted wood, the lawn, the bowling-green, the terrace, the many walks, the little knoll.

Mr Rushworth, silly though he may be, is not irresponsible: he wishes to 'improve' his house and estate. To 'improve' involves making changes that will add to the value of the property, but the word had a particular significance in Jane Austen's day of creating a 'picturesque' or apparently natural effect. To achieve this, formal features were removed, ponds and rivers artificially added; the architecture and interior decoration of the house might also be altered. But change, for Jane Austen and for Fanny, must be organic, not destructive: Fanny deplored Mr Rushworth's plan to fell the beautiful straight avenue of oaks.

Henry Crawford, so full of ideas and 'improvements' for other peoples' estates, betrays his irresponsibility by the neglect of his own. He comes nearest to good sense when he talks to Fanny in Portsmouth (Chapter 41) about his estate, his new-found interest in his tenants and his suspicions of his agent. He plans to go to Everingham, but never gets there: his neglect of his estate leads directly to the reunion with Maria and the loss of Fanny.

Duty and decorum

The twin ideas of duty and decorum are fundamental to the pattern of life in a house such as Mansfield Park, representative of good English society. Duty to one's parents (in which Tom consistently fails and even Edmund wavers during the theatricals); duty to one's dependents; duty to one's descendants, in preserving their heritage.

The harmony of the house depends on decorum, the sense of what is fitting, which is used as a touchstone throughout the novel. Decorum is lacking in the Price household, but ever-present at Mansfield Park under Sir Thomas's rule. Decorum is the sense of propriety which should prevent young ladies from acting at all, let alone in the dubious *Lovers' Vows*, as Edmund tells Maria. It encompasses all matters, from accepting an invitation to placing the furniture. The first threat to decorum in Mansfield Park is the moving of Sir Thomas's bookcase, the disarrangement of his study spreading to the disruption of the whole house, which Sir Thomas, on his return, has to restore 'to its proper state'. Maria's elopement, thinks Fanny, will fall most horribly on Sir Thomas's 'high sense of honour and decorum'. The link between decorum and duty is apparent in his agonised realisation that he has failed in his duty towards his daughters by not teaching them *their* duties. Mary Crawford, with her indecorous remarks about her uncle, her outspoken conversation and irreverent views, flouts decorum, while Fanny upholds it.

Rank and money

Rank and money are what matters in a society such as that of Mansfield Park: both involve responsibilities as well as 'consequence'. Both preserve the fabric of society, and it is foolhardy to discount them. In marriage, especially, it is one's duty to aim as high as one can, unlike the imprudent Mrs Price.

The social standing of the main characters ranges from the undesirable Mr Price to Sir Thomas Bertram, who is a baronet, that is, a member of the hereditary aristocracy, though of its lowest rank. Sir Thomas is a Member of Parliament, and had kept a London house until Lady Bertram's indolence caused him to give it up. 'The Bertrams are undoubtedly some of the first people in the county'(Northamptonshire), with Sir Thomas's daughters among its leading belles. Mr Rushworth and Mr Crawford are wealthy but not titled: Mr Yates is the son of an Earl, but not, alas, an elder son, therefore merely 'the Honourable John Yates', and never to be a Lord.

The question of the title, which the eldest son inherits along with the family estate and money, teases Mary Crawford. She first sets her sights on Tom Bertram, who will, when his father dies, become 'the Sir Thomas complete, which he was to be in time'. It is 'very vexatious' for her to fall in love with Edmund. She refers frequently to names and titles, and does not wish to sink under the 'annihilation' of an untitled marriage. She spells this out in her very tasteless letter to Fanny (Chapter 45) in which she speculates on Tom's possible death. She can barter her money for a title; Mrs Grant has already fixed on Tom Bertram for her: 'the eldest son of a Baronet was not too good for a girl of twenty thousand pounds.'

Money is openly discussed in the novel. Mary Crawford has her capital of twenty thousand pounds; Lady Bertram made a very good match on only seven thousand pounds. Of the men, Henry Crawford has four thousand pounds a year, much less than Mr Rushworth with twelve thousand pounds a year; but how much more than poor Edmund, who must work for his income, which Crawford calculates will be seven hundred pounds a year from his 'living' or parish. Mary Crawford is not displeased that her brother Henry should consider marrying beneath him, because she herself will be making a bad match financially if she marries Edmund.

Marriage

The aspects of marriage debated in *Mansfield Park* are those of material, intellectual and emotional compatibility. It mattered greatly to marry within one's own class, preferably above one's own position in it. Mary Crawford asserts that 'every body should marry as soon as they can do it to advantage'. Maria, early in the novel, is 'beginning to think matrimony a duty'. Mr Rushworth's eligibility rests on his land and his money: only Edmund observes that 'if this man had not twelve thousand a year, he would be a very stupid fellow'. Sir Thomas allows the financial side of the marriage to weigh against Maria's coldness towards Mr Rushworth. Mr Crawford is presented to Fanny as an ideal match, for the money, rank, and position he would offer her; Lady Bertram tells her that 'it is every young woman's duty to accept such a very unexceptionable offer' and even Edmund thinks it 'most advantageous and desirable', adding 'if you could return his affection', for he sees the need for emotional attachment. He also advocates intellectual compatibility, telling Fanny that she and Henry Crawford have 'moral and literary tastes in common'. Her seriousness and his liveliness will counterbalance each other, and her firmness will steady him. Edmund's own longed-for marriage with Mary Crawford would be such a combination of opposites, he thinks: he would guide her away from the bad influences that might corrupt her mind, while enjoying her brilliance and beauty. When he and Fanny finally marry, it is similarity, not differences between them, that brings their perfect happiness.

Many bitter things are said about marriage in the course of the novel. Mary Crawford cynically observes that 'there is not one in a hundred of either sex who is not taken in when they marry'. Maria marries only for the freedom from restriction and discipline she enjoyed while her father was away. This reason, however harshly put, is a comment on the position of women at the time, who had no independence. While they were at home unmarried, they were strictly chaperoned and their freedom severely restricted. A woman of good breeding who had no money could not take a job except as a governess or (badly) paid companion. It was therefore important to marry for security – though a woman's own money went to her husband when she married. Once she was married, she still had to observe decorum. Maria's misbehaviour with Mr Crawford is considered serious enough to get into the newspapers. Very few people would treat adultery as lightly as Mary Crawford: although divorce was legal, Sir Thomas could not let Maria re-enter local society.

The Church

Jane Austen was very familiar with the Church, many members of her family, including her father, having been clergymen. In this novel, she shows two views of the clergy: that of Henry and Mary Crawford, belittling; that of Sir Thomas Bertram, Edmund and Fanny, elevated. Many of the clergymen in her novels (such as Mr Elton in *Emma*) seem worldly; Edmund is not. At the time, livings or parishes belonged to and were 'in the gift of' private families. Hence Sir Thomas presented Mr Norris with the living of Mansfield, which on his death would have been kept for Edmund by a temporary incumbent, but for Tom's debts. Sir Thomas had another living to offer, however, that of Thornton Lacey; Mary Crawford suggests that Edmund has chosen the church only because he has a living waiting for him. She sees no distinction in the profession. To her, 'a clergyman is nothing', whereas Edmund sees him as having 'the charge of all that is of the first importance to mankind'.

Henry Crawford thinks a clergyman need only preach occasionally, and does not expect Edmund to live in his parish, but Sir Thomas and Edmund think that if a clergyman does not live among his parishioners 'and prove himself by constant attention their well-wisher and friend, he does very little either for their good or his own'.

Religion as a guide to behaviour and morals is a force in the novel, noted sometimes for its absence: Sir Thomas, reflecting on his daughters' lack of moral purpose, says 'They had been instructed theoretically in their religion, but never required to bring it into daily practice.' In the chapel at Sotherton, Mary Crawford sneers at 'the good people who used to kneel and gape in that gallery . . . starched up into seeming piety', whereas to Fanny 'a whole family assembling regularly for the purpose of prayer, is fine!' – and she staunchly supports religion and the clerical ideal throughout the novel.

Plot

The main plot of *Mansfield Park* is that of Fanny Price's development from immaturity to maturity. There are three aspects of Fanny's development, which might also be seen as separate plots: in relationship with Mansfield Park and its inhabitants; in relationship with Edmund Bertram; in relationship with Henry Crawford. But they can all be reduced to the single plot of Fanny's relationship with herself: her acceptance of herself and of her own importance. In counterpoint to the Fanny–Mansfield Park plot stands that of Fanny's separation from her own home in Portsmouth; in counterpoint to the Fanny–Edmund plot stands that of Edmund's infatuation with Mary Crawford. In counterpoint to the Fanny–Henry Crawford plot we find the multiple one of Henry Crawford and the Bertram sisters – his double entanglement, their rivalry, Maria's marriage, and her elopement with him.

Structure

The shifting structure

The structure of the novel is dictated by its plot and is dislocated where the plot is dislocated. The movement of the first part (Chapters 1–18) is that of a group, gathering, forming, re-forming, working towards the theatrical performance which never takes place. The patterns made within this group are significant, but shifting, with Fanny often alone, set apart outside the main group. At the dramatic but anticlimactic reappearance of Sir Thomas, the group movement of the 'theatricals' stops short and is never resolved. The pattern is left in suspension, the group frozen into immobility, with Henry Crawford holding Maria's hand, before the group disperses, never to come together again.

The next 'section' of the structure (Chapters 19–37) is constructed round Fanny's courtship by Mr Crawford and the tension between these two characters; Fanny is now in the foreground at Mansfield Park, after Maria's marriage and her departure with Julia. An echoing yet contrasting pattern is that of Edmund's courtship of Miss Crawford, muted by being shown only indirectly through Edmund's confidences to Fanny. We are aware of the links between these two pairs, reinforced by Fanny's feeling of dependence on the outcome of Edmund's affair with Miss Crawford, her reluctant yet fascinated intimacy with Miss Crawford, and her position as confidante of both.

A further dislocation occurs when Fanny goes to Portsmouth (Chapters 38–46). Now the immediate tension is between Fanny and her home circle, and in her realisation that Mansfield Park is her true home. But the structure of the novel almost disintegrates with regard to the other plots, as Fanny receives only irregular and incomplete information by letter. Whereas the first two sections contain much direct speech, with both sides of the conversations fully recorded, we now have only indirect reports of Fanny's conversations with her mother and Susan. The fragmentary nature of the information received prevents this section having a regular and satisfying shape, either in itself or in relation to the rest of the novel. It also affects our perceptions of what is actually happening, and of the characters. While Fanny is considering marrying Henry Crawford to make a home for Susan, he is in Richmond preparing to elope with Maria – which we, and Fanny, must work out from letters and even the newspaper. This creates a deep and disturbing irony.

After the long wait for Sir Thomas, Edmund's hasty arrival to take Fanny back to Mansfield Park leaves the pattern broken or non-existent (in itself a statement of lack of harmony and order). It is noticeable that Fanny does not come to any conclusive relationship with her family: she plucks Susan from it as she and William have already been plucked, but (despite her own guilty feelings) her parents are indifferent, sealed off from the rest of the characters by their lack of curiosity as much as by distance. The dénouement emphasises the novel's shifting perspective. Long spans of time are briefly despatched or left undefined. The narrator steps in to sort matters out, impatient to restore those not greatly at fault to 'tolerable comfort', and to 'have done with all the rest'. Harmony is restored cursorily: Mary Crawford's life is dismissed in a few lines, Henry Crawford's motives, his entanglement with Maria, their life together and their separation briefly outlined, and even the love and marriage of Fanny and Edmund merely sketched.

Episodes

There are four major episodes in the novel: the outing to Sotherton; the theatricals; Henry Crawford's courtship of Fanny; her trip to Portsmouth. These episodes are more self-contained, more distinct from their surroundings, than elements of the plot such as Fanny's love for Edmund or his for Mary Crawford, which are woven into the novel.

Sotherton
Up to the visit to Sotherton, the characters of the book have been assembling (only Mr Yates is yet to appear). With Sir Thomas away the general grouping has been that of the Bertrams, Grants, Crawfords and Rushworths together, with Fanny on the outside, looking on. Sometimes she is with Edmund, but very often, as when the young people are riding and Mary Crawford has the mare, Fanny is quite alone. At Sotherton there is a radical regrouping of the characters. Maria and Henry Crawford form a unit (as she has never done with Mr Rushworth); Edmund is paired openly with Mary Crawford, with Fanny occasionally an uncomfortable 'third', but even more isolated in that capacity. She is still the observant outsider, but is placed in an intriguing position as the others come to talk to her while she sits on her bench. It is at Sotherton that she faces her own feelings for Edmund, her misery at being abandoned by him and her 'disappointment and depression' at his interest in Mary Crawford.

The theatricals
Between the visit to Sotherton and the return of Sir Thomas, the novel is entirely taken up with the theatricals. Edmund is at first ranged 'with' Fanny against the performers but then coupled with Mary Crawford by their roles in the play. Maria and Henry Crawford very ostentatiously display themselves as a pair, with Mr Rushworth ineffectually in the wings. Julia's only contact with the group is Mr Yates, to whom she comments acidly on the acting. Mrs Norris takes part busily in the group; Lady Bertram is physically present (though mentally absent). This episode marks a distinct stage in Fanny's becoming an individual: standing alone against the theatricals, she displays moral courage and self-assertion for the first time. The theatricals show everyone except Fanny in a sort of reversion to childhood; civilised manners and formal conventions are abandoned, as they march out in a temper (like Julia), angle for partners (like Mary Crawford and Maria), demand the best parts, or selfishly seek a play to suit themselves.

Henry Crawford's courtship of Fanny
Henry Crawford's determined wooing of Fanny (Chapters 24–36) can be judged an episode as much as a relationship. Unlike the other

courtships, which are woven into the texture of the novel, this one is an adventure which Henry Crawford invents, announcing to his sister his plan 'to make Fanny Price in love with me', and later 'to marry Fanny Price'. The actor in Henry Crawford makes him do all the right things – look for news of William's ship, help him towards promotion, declare himself, propose to Fanny, ask Sir Thomas's permission and assistance, persevere in spite of her refusal. But we know that these are merely acts in the drama of 'Henry Crawford, the irresistible lover', and that it is her opposition that attracts him. We learn in the final chapter that Fanny has been the one woman, 'whom he had rationally, as well as passionately loved', led on, ironically, by his own performance.

Henry Crawford does help Fanny towards maturity by recognising that she is no longer a child; he makes her realise her own value – she will not accept him merely because he proposes: 'How then was I to be – to be in love with him the moment he was with me?' She even stands up to Sir Thomas's severe reprimand with 'I cannot like him, Sir, well enough to marry him.' And in the last scene of his courtship, Henry Crawford's visit to Portsmouth helps her to understand that she needs sophistication, elegance and grace, not necessarily in a husband, but in the society around her.

Portsmouth

Fanny's attainment of adulthood is directly linked with her stay in Portsmouth, astutely planned by Sir Thomas to make her 'heartily sick of home before her visit ended'. One of her original sources of misery is that she misses 'the brothers and sisters among whom she had always been important as play-fellow, instructress and nurse', and in her mind the idea of importance and a place within society remains fixed on Portsmouth. When she returns there, however, she is a stranger, her parents are indifferent, she is stunned by the noise, and above all she feels shy of helping or giving: 'so unpractised in removing evils, or bestowing kindnesses among her equals, and so fearful of appearing to elevate herself' that she can scarcely bring herself to buy the knife for Betsey. She does assert herself by educating Susan, and soon afterwards realises that her role is to help and support, not here but at Mansfield Park, not as an inferior, but as an equal.

Signs and symbols

Mansfield Park contains three very effective examples of the use of certain events to suggest deeper feelings, emotions or thoughts. They are: the passing over the locked gate to the park at Sotherton (Chapter 10), the theatricals (Chapters 13–18), and the game of Speculation (Chapter 25). The crossing of the iron gate by Maria and Mr Crawford is sexually suggestive, prefiguring their adultery. When Maria complains that 'that iron gate, that ha-ha, give me a feeling of restraint and hardship', Mr Crawford replies that she could 'with little difficulty pass round the edge of the gate, here, with my assistance', hinting that she would not wish to do so 'without the key and without Mr Rushworth's authority and protection' (representing her legitimate access to sexuality via her marriage and her husband). The trespass affects Julia: she pushes past, determined to follow, just as she later emulates Maria's elopement. Fanny is outside the gate throughout, sitting on her bench, while Edmund and Mary Crawford stroll through the delightful glades and avenues that she desires to reach. We cannot avoid seeing a parallel with Maria's more openly sexual exploits.

The theatricals bear an equal weight of suggestion (see the section on 'Episodes' above, pp. 48–9). There is the constant rehearsing, and hence intimacy, not only of Henry Crawford and Maria Bertram, but of Edmund and Mary Crawford as well; as she has previously put it so bluntly, 'Who is to be Anhalt? What gentleman among you am I to have the pleasure of making love to?' Poor Fanny, caught with them as prompter and critic, becomes 'agitated' by the 'increasing spirit of Edmund's manner' as Amelia–Mary talks to him of love and marriage. The theatricals are the outward and visible signs of an inward and spiritual disorder at Mansfield Park.

The game of Speculation is also indicative of the deeper feelings of those concerned, revealing their characters and intimating what is going on behind their social masks. Henry Crawford, attentive to Lady Bertram yet concentrating all his charm on Fanny, teaches and guides her in a parody of the teaching and guidance she had received from Edmund. He wants to teach her to be hard, to will herself to win. Edmund, more sensitive to her true nature, observes that she would much rather give the game to William. Mary Crawford, on the other hand, is determined to win at any price: 'If I lose the game, it shall not be from not striving for it'. She wins: 'The game was her's and only did not pay her for what she had given to secure it.' Her state of mind is equally relevant to the discussion of Edmund's new parish that is going on at the same time as the game: as Sir Thomas and Edmund expatiate on the clergyman's duty, 'all the agreeable of *her* speculation was over for that hour.' In the outcome of the novel Mary Crawford does in fact pay too high a price, for immediate pleasures (of London) and for frivolity (concerning the elopement) and loses Edmund.

Characterisation

Jane Austen's characterisation in *Mansfield Park* is marked by (*a*) an elaborate series of parallels and contrasts, (*b*) by the observation of each character within relationships that swiftly change and develop (and are themselves paralleled and contrasted) and (c) by the splendid variety of its cast.

Parallels and contrasts

A very elaborate system of parallels and contrasts forms a network throughout the book. The main polarity is between the 'characters' of Mansfield Park and the Price house in Portsmouth (and behind the two, of the civilised country society of Northamptonshire and the coarse one of Portsmouth). There are straightforward contrasts to be drawn between people such as the responsible, high-minded Sir Thomas and the negligent Mr Price, or the high-principled Edmund, constant and honourable, and the inconstant and insincere Henry Crawford. A contrast can be perceived between Edmund, the younger son, and the careless, spendthrift elder son, Tom. Fanny is seen in contrast with the confident Maria and Julia, and later with the frivolous Mary Crawford. Other more complex parallels are drawn between more than two characters: the three former Misses Ward, for example.

Equally revealing are the parallels and contrasts between people's relationships. That between Fanny and Edmund, founded on mutual tenderness and respect, is altogether different from Henry Crawford's impetuous, self-willed and insincere would-be relationship with Fanny. And in its turn we compare the latter with Henry Crawford's relationship with Maria, bred of flirting and vanity. This relationship invites comparison with the worldly alliance between Maria and Mr Rushworth, while the slowly-maturing relationship between Edmund and Fanny is also contrasted with Edmund's swift infatuation with Mary Crawford. She plays with him and teases him, but Edmund wishes to 'educate' her just as he has educated Fanny, not seeing that the relationships are as different as the two women's characters and behaviour.

Relationships

Character is revealed throughout the novel under the stress of certain relationships. Maria and Julia, at first a polished pair of society belles, reflecting each other's elegance, are turned by their relationships with Henry Crawford into ill-tempered, spiteful rivals, who both appear foolish and ill-bred. Mary Crawford, in her relationship with Edmund, is seen at first merely as 'a young woman, pretty, lively, with a harp as elegant as herself', but as the relationship deepens she becomes more outspoken, more irreverent. While he tries to educate and elevate her, she becomes more unyielding, more worldly, more corrupt, eventually betraying her amorality through her attitude to the elopement.

Fanny's own relationships shift throughout the novel. That with Edmund is unswerving, but she herself develops from his pupil to his confidante to his equal. Her relationship with Henry Crawford on the other hand is uncertain, her emotions veering from indifference to dislike to gratitude to resentment to respect (at Portsmouth) and finally to scorn and disgust. It is not only the love relationships that shift and develop: Fanny's relationship with Sir Thomas moves from reserve (caused by her timidity) to mutual respect (on his return from Antigua) to estrangement and resentment (when she refuses Henry Crawford) to final reconciliation. Fanny's relationship with Mary Crawford is also a shifting one. Based on mistrust on Fanny's side, it yet becomes a strange tripartite one with Edmund. When he is away, it becomes curiously intimate. Fanny's mistrust is re-awakened by Miss Crawford's letters to Portsmouth, and vindicated when the latter condones Maria's adultery.

The cast: characters in *Mansfield Park*

Fanny

Many saccharine adjectives are applied to Fanny Price by the narrator and the other characters – 'sweet', 'pretty', 'quiet', 'gentle', 'modest', 'timid', 'shy', 'graceful'. None of these describes the true Fanny, who is clever, observant, strong-minded and practical. But until she herself accepts the positive, active part of her nature, she cannot fill her place at Mansfield or in society. We learn early on that much may be hidden beneath 'her quiet passive manner', which can conceal constant terror and nightly sobbing. If it is Edmund who unlocks her feelings (both at this early point and later by inspiring her love), it is also he who draws out her intellectual faculties, knowing her 'to be clever, to have a quick apprehension ... and fondness for reading'. And it is Edmund who understands her need to be important and her capacity to be so: 'There is no reason in the world why you should not be important where you are known. You have good sense, and a sweet temper, and I am sure you have a grateful heart.' Only he sees the good sense, everyone else merely imposing on the sweet temper and grateful heart. Fanny herself has to learn to have faith in her own good sense, and to develop the strength to transmit it to others. During the theatricals, she sees the impropriety of what the others are doing, but although she behaves correctly herself, she is incapable of imposing her opinions on them – even on Edmund. It is she who sees that Henry Crawford is trifling with Maria and Julia: she braces herself to tell Edmund, but again is not forceful enough to impose her views. It is not until she reassesses her own abilities in Portsmouth that she realises that she is capable of seeing and judging correctly, of giving, of being positively useful. The early Fanny is too wrapped up in her own position as an outsider to take her proper place. Her withdrawals to her own East room are in one way acts of strength, in another of weakness – of too much reserve, of an unwillingness to integrate herself into the family, although by this time she loves Mansfield Park 'and every thing in it'. The 'persuadableness' which Sir Thomas sees as a virtue is not wholly admirable: she herself compares her 'supine and yielding temper' unfavourably with Susan's determination. Edmund urges her to conquer the diffidence which prevents her good qualities being seen, and comments on her 'disposition to be easily dejected, and to fancy difficulties greater than they are'. It is not until she has overcome these faults, while retaining the positive side of her nature, that she can take her rightful place as mistress of Mansfield parsonage.

Mary Crawford

Mary Crawford, however sparkling, lively, charming or witty she may appear, is ruthlessly determined to dominate. With her twenty thousand pounds and her 'true London maxim, that every thing is to be got for money', she feels she can buy what she cannot charm. Setbacks, such as her discovery that her influence has not altered Edmund's determination to become a clergyman, make her angry and vengeful: 'she would henceforth admit his attentions without any idea beyond immediate amusement.' Her desire to dominate is articulated when she speaks of Fanny's conquest of Henry Crawford: 'the glory of fixing one who has been shot at by so many'.

With this to contend with, Edmund's notion that he can guide her into the light is ironic, as is his talk of her 'little errors' or 'tinge of wrong', and indeed his assertion 'I have never been blinded.' He thinks at one point that 'She does not think evil, but she speaks it – speaks it in playfulness,' and it is a long time before he can say 'my eyes are opened' and talk of her 'corrupt, vitiated mind'. Many notions of darkness and blindness cling to Mary Crawford, in contrast with her early brilliance and her consistent lightness. Fanny sees 'a mind led astray and bewildered, and without any suspicion of being so; darkened, yet fancying itself light'. The triumph of Fanny over her opposite, Mary Crawford, is the triumph of spiritual light over the powers of darkness.

Lady Bertram

Lady Bertram is beautiful, and she is indolent. She has allowed these two qualities to take over her character, and to submerge all other feelings and features, which appear only occasionally, as when her husband returns from Antigua, or under the stress of Tom's grave illness, when she nurses him, writes daily to Fanny and is in every way galvanised into activity. It is a measure of Fanny's final integration into Mansfield Park that when she returns from Portsmouth Lady Bertram actually comes out to meet her, 'with no indolent step'.

Lady Bertram is too boring even to talk over the ball; she is too stupid to play Speculation. Although she is fond of her husband, she is neither alert nor sensitive enough to be afraid for him when he is in the West Indies. In her indolence she abdicates her role as mistress of the house and as mother, allowing Mrs Norris to chaperone Maria and Julia to balls, to choose an unsuitable husband for Maria, and to have far too large a hand in their education, as Sir Thomas eventually sees.

Her beauty is her other dominating feature. Because it has enabled her to marry well, it has directed her life, and she feels it is every woman's duty to take up a good offer if her beauty brings her one: 'Beauty and wealth were all that excited her respect'. Mr Crawford's proposal 'by convincing her that Fanny *was* very pretty, which she had been doubting about before, and that she would be advantageously married ... made her feel a sort of credit in calling her niece'. To have 'a handsome family' is the height of her ambition, with no thought of inward grace or spiritual beauty.

Mrs Norris

Mrs Norris is one of Jane Austen's great comic creations, but nevertheless a somewhat sinister character. She is on the surface the soul of energy and honest work, the guardian of her nieces, their mentor, their defender. But as Sir Thomas realises in the end, she is also their destroyer – her education is not towards moral probity but towards appearances and materialism. She has obtruded between father and daughters by 'teaching them to repress their spirits in his presence' and to 'make their real disposition unknown to him'. She treats Fanny, on the other hand, with unremitting severity.

She is determined to control everything, from Maria's choice of husband to whether or not Sir Thomas will take soup on his return. It is not her place to make such decisions; moreover, whereas Sir Thomas governs liberally and kindly, Mrs Norris is dictatorial and petty, mean enough to quibble over a meal for the carpenter's son. She loses sight of the greater issues in her concentration on the lesser, being too much occupied 'contriving and directing the general little matters of the company' to see the impropriety of their play, too busy, 'saving, with delighted integrity, half-a-crown here and there to the absent Sir Thomas, to have leisure for watching the behaviour, or guarding the happiness of his daughters'.

Maria Bertram

At first indistinguishable from her sister Julia in robust self-confidence and social skills, Maria soon emerges as the leading sister – not merely in age but in enterprise as well. She snatches the leading role in the play, and gets her revenge for Julia's journey to Sotherton on the box with Mr Crawford by flirting with him there. She is the first favourite with Mrs Norris, the first engaged, the first to cross the iron gate into the forbidden territory. Her flirtatious exchanges with Mr Crawford are brief but very intense. She leads, rather than merely responding to him, both in the chapel and at the locked gate that gives her such a sense of 'hardship and restraint'. This intolerance of restriction is her most distinctive trait: her readiness for marriage springs from 'a hatred of home, restraint and tranquillity'. She is a 'finished' product of society yet has no understanding of its duties: having entered into a contract with Mr Rushworth she has not the integrity to abide by it, only feeling a momentary possessive interest in Sotherton when she can show it off to her friends. Her 'anxious and expensive education', as her father finally realises, has taught her only the superficialities of life, without the duty, discipline or decorum that are its backbone.

Julia Bertram

Julia, like her sister Maria, is a product of an education directed towards accomplishments rather than morals. Her father sees at the end of the novel that the combination of his strictness and Mrs Norris's indulgence has bred that deceitfulness which, combined with the prospect of increased restrictions at home after Maria's elopement, allows Julia to run away with Mr Yates. Unlike Maria's, her part in her affair is a passive one – though a girl with steadfast moral purpose would not have yielded. Julia, like Maria, is too bound up in her own pleasure to go home to comfort Lady Bertram during Tom's illness; she is too selfish to befriend her cousin Fanny; too petulant to take her rebuff from Henry Crawford with dignity. Able to sing, play, dance and converse, she, like Maria, is 'entirely deficient in the less common acquirements of self-knowledge, generosity and humility'.

Susan

Appearing late in the novel, Susan throws an interesting light on Fanny: we realise that it is not only Fanny's 'sensibility' that raises her above the level of her Portsmouth home. Susan, who has endured more years of it than Fanny, deplores and fights against the sluttishness, dirt and noise of the house. Her temper, which Fanny at first regards as impossible to tame, is the result of the friction between her view of how things should be done and the reality of the Price household. Susan proves an eager learner from Fanny (as Fanny has been from Edmund). She has many of the qualities that Fanny eventually achieves – the initiative to act unbidden (when she first produces tea for Fanny after her journey), common sense in helping her brothers and sisters, and an ease of manner that helps her to put up with indifference, hostility from Mrs Norris, and being 'left a good deal to herself' at Mansfield Park.

Mrs Price

The unfortunate and imprudent third sister is an object lesson in how not to marry, how not to run a house, how not to behave, how not to bring up one's family – 'a dawdle, a slattern, who neither taught nor restrained her children'. She has 'no talent, no conversation, no affection towards [Fanny]; no curiosity to know her better, no desire of her friendship, and no inclination for her company that could lessen her sense of such feelings'. But it is clear that all these deficiencies spring from her original mistake and mismarriage. Mr Price's lack of means and gentility wreak havoc on his wife; it grieves Fanny to think of the contrast between her mother and Lady Bertram. This is the obverse side of Fanny's conviction that one should marry for love, not for money.

Mrs Grant

Mary Crawford's idea of the perfect wife, Mrs Grant is subservient to a greedy, self-indulgent and irritable man fifteen years her senior. She good-humouredly keeps a good table and employs an expensive cook for him, stays in when he is unwell, weathers his rage at a 'green goose', worries about getting the turkey to table in good condition, and even has the tact to leave the cook in total charge of her own domain. She is in other words the pattern of a good ministering wife. Her marriage, however, is not very rewarding for this woman 'of a temper to love and be loved'. A marriage like hers lacks that equality and affinity that Fanny eventually finds with Edmund, in, ironically, that same parsonage in which Mrs Grant coped so self-abnegatingly with Dr Grant.

Mrs Rushworth

'A well-meaning, civil, prosing, pompous woman', Mrs Rushworth is the personification of society in this novel. Judging only by externals, she helps Mrs Norris in her matchmaking, not from any officiousness on her part, but from total devotion to her son and his happiness. She does all the right things, showing Sotherton to its best advantage, moving out of it to cede her place to the new Mrs Rushworth, Maria. It is therefore natural that when her daughter-in-law commits adultery and elopes with Henry Crawford, she should be hostile and bitter. 'The personal disrespect with which she had herself been treated' is an almost equal offence against propriety. This well-mannered, well-connected dowager becomes 'unmanageable', representing, in her antagonism, the whole of affronted society.

Edmund

Fanny's friend, supporter and teacher, it is Edmund who first takes pity on Fanny, first sees that she is clever, and first develops her mind. He also cares for her physical well-being, providing her with a horse for exercise, worrying about her headaches. 'With his strong good sense and uprightness of mind' he is Fanny's pillar of strength and comfort: 'Edmund's friendship never failed her.'

We see therefore with amazement Edmund turning unreasonable and thoughtless under the influence of Mary Crawford. He allows her to monopolise the mare obtained for Fanny's use, and goes off on riding parties with her and the others for several days running, abandoning Fanny to her demanding aunts. He also surprisingly discounts Fanny's worries about Maria and Julia and Henry Crawford, and allows himself to be talked into taking part in the theatricals to please Miss Crawford. Despite all temptations, however, Edmund never loses sight of his duty as a clergyman, taking an unusually dedicated and spiritual view of it, which mortifies Miss Crawford, but endears him to Fanny.

His love for Fanny, unlike his infatuation with Mary Crawford, springs from 'a regard founded on the most endearing claims of innocence and helplessness'. It is not, however, until he has turned to *her* for comfort that this love comes to life: their early relationship is reversed; he is the child, she the parent – his guide, comforter and friend.

Henry Crawford

Henry Crawford is mercurial to the point of wishing his own personality and situation away: when William talks, he wants to be a sailor, when listening to Edmund he wants to become a clergyman. He is able to talk to everyone in turn about their interests, and this ability to lose his true self makes him such a remarkably fine actor: even while Fanny deplores the theatricals, she admires his acting; when she distrusts him most, she is enthralled by his reading of Shakespeare. His inability to stop acting makes it virtually impossible for him to have an honest relationship with anybody except his sister, with whom he is almost too honest. It is to her that he explains his feelings for Maria and Julia, and later for Fanny. It is always the challenge that fires him – Maria being almost at the altar with Mr Rushworth, Fanny's grave looks. He has no respect for women: he wants Fanny to 'feel when I go away that she shall be never happy again'; he 'destroys' Maria's happiness unthinkingly. He carries his 'great dislike' of 'any thing like a permanence of abode, or limitation of society' into his dealings with women, with the lack of constancy that Fanny perceives. The perseverance in pursuit of Fanny which Sir Thomas finds so impressive is not constancy, but merely an assertion of his vanity, which refuses to accept that his charm has failed. For charm he undoubtedly has: his sister tells Fanny of the numerous conquests he has made; the narrator gives him credit for 'air and countenance' and a splendid manner; and even Fanny in Portsmouth admires his urbane wit: 'such a man could come from no place, no society, without importing something to amuse.' But behind these superficial graces, we are always aware of the corrupt cynicism that allows him to oust and cuckold Mr Rushworth, to trifle with Maria and Julia, and to destroy the customary peace of Mansfield Park.

Thomas Bertram

Tom is characterised by the happy selfishness with which he looks upon the sacrifice of Edmund's living to his extravagant ways: 'the younger brother must help to pay for the pleasures of the elder.' His pleasures are hinted at throughout the novel – there are signs before his illness that he lives a dissolute life. His vices spring from his being the elder brother and heir: without effort or worth on his part, the family's house, estate and money are destined for him.

During the theatricals Tom shows considerable force of character, in instigating and carrying through the plans, and in overcoming Edmund's objections. His use of his energies in this way is, of course, unprofitable and wasteful: he shows no sign of helping his father with either estate or business. We hear that during his illness he learns to suffer and to think, and that he becomes 'what he ought to be, useful to his father, steady and quiet, and not living merely for himself'; but we never see this at first hand, and it is not at all like the Tom we know.

Sir Thomas Bertram

Sir Thomas, 'master at Mansfield Park', seems to be the epitome of sense and good management: he runs his house and estate with scrupulous attention to detail. He is a devoted husband, a careful and dutiful father. He is lofty and dignified. Yet despite these virtues, he has, in the course of the novel, two daughters lost by elopement, one son near death from dissipation, another infatuated with an amoral woman, a niece whom he tries to marry to a rake, and an indolent wife and interfering sister-in-law who between them allow the family to drift into misbehaviour. Why?

It would be wrong to attribute all the disturbances in Mansfield Park to the Crawfords. The weaknesses are already within it, and Sir Thomas himself attributes them to his own blindness. Concerned only with the outward forms, he has taken infinite care of his daughters' education in accomplishments but not in morals; has had them taught religion but not its practice; has 'meant them to be good', but has not directed them to self-denial, humility, or duty. 'Something must have been wanting *within.*' Much of the inner weakness at Mansfield Park has come through Mrs Norris, who has, by undue indulgence counteracting his severity, encouraged Maria and Julia to conceal their true natures from their father: but he sees very well at the end that it is he who has allowed Mrs Norris free rein. He has delegated his moral responsibility to her as cavalierly as Lady Bertram.

Many of Sir Thomas's good and weak points can be seen in his dealings with Fanny. He is kind enough to take her in, responsible enough to consider the implications both financial and personal; yet too stern and unbending to make her happy. He seems kinder and more tender to her when he comes back from Antigua, yet his 'good opinion' evaporates when she refuses Henry Crawford and she grieves to hear his 'accusations, so heavy, so multiplied, so rising in dreadful gradation'. In the end, punished by the dreadful blows that have struck his family, he welcomes her as a daughter-in-law, at last 'sick of ambitious and mercenary connections' which have endangered his house and family.

Mr Rushworth

Mr Rushworth in his pink satin cloak is a cipher. Pitted against the strong, unscrupulous Mr Crawford, he is virtually invisible, and as Maria cuts down his speeches in the play, so she cuts down his importance in real life. Although Mr Rushworth has money, family, and 'one of the largest estates and finest places in the country', he has not the character to go with them. He represents the less admirable side of the upper classes, without the sense or administrative ability of Sir Thomas. He does not live up to the noble character of his house, having no sense of his duty to preserve the past. Sotherton is beautifully kept, but certain traditions (such as the holding of family service in the chapel) have lapsed, and his determination to 'improve' it entails destroying some of its finest features . This 'heavy young man, with not more than common sense', allows Maria to treat him badly, never standing up to her, although he does show his jealousy of Mr Crawford by criticising his acting. His own vanity is soon assuaged by his fine costume for the play. We cannot feel too sorry for him; indeed we are directed not to: 'the indignities of stupidity, and the disappointments of selfish passion, can excite little pity.'

Mr Yates

Mr Yates is a lesser Henry Crawford. Rich (but not so rich); an actor (but not such a good one); a would-be seducer (but without Henry Crawford's successes to boast of). Even his elopement is not such a disaster as Maria's – he turns out to be a fairly good match after all, the son of an earl, 'desirous of being equally received into the family', and disposed to look up to Sir Thomas. 'He was not very solid; but there was a hope of his becoming less trifling – of his being at least tolerably domestic and quiet,' and above all, his estate proves to be 'rather more', and his debts 'much less' than Sir Thomas feared. That is the last we hear of Mr Yates and Julia.

Mr Yates means most to us during the theatricals, when his ranting makes itself heard incessantly. The comedy of his rehearsing all over the house is irresistible. When, insensitive to the Crawford's suggestion that he leave the Bertrams alone for the evening of Sir Thomas's return, he betrays the theatricals to Sir Thomas by his loud orations, he is quite without suspicion that his host might be displeased. But despite all the comedy inherent in Mr Yates, one realises that he is a disturber of the peace, an unsettling influence. He would not have been invited for such a long time had Sir Thomas not been absent – he is one of the 'hundred best friends' from whom Sir Thomas takes Tom away.

Dr Grant

Dr Grant is a negative, contrary man. He is the opposite of his young, gay, extrovert wife; as clergyman he is the opposite of the dedicated Edmund; the opposite kind of husband from Sir Thomas, who looks after everyone belonging to him – Dr Grant needs constant looking-after himself. He has, according to Mary Crawford's first view, the air of a gentleman, but when she has lived in his house she revises her opinion of him: 'I see him to be an indolent, selfish bon vivant, who must have his palate consulted in every thing, who will not stir a finger for the convenience of any one.' His bad temper and over-indulgence make it fitting that, having risen in the Church, he should 'bring on apoplexy and death, by three great institutionary dinners in one week'.

William

William forms a constant link in the novel between Fanny and her own background; it is William whom she first thinks of, talks of and writes to. It is William too who first calls out the warm, affectionate, confiding side of her nature which she blocks for so long at Mansfield Park. The fresh enthusiastic midshipman charms everyone – the jaded Henry Crawford, the dignified Sir Thomas Bertram. He need only mention his promotion for the former to arrange it for him; he need only observe that he has never seen Fanny dance for Sir Thomas to arrange a ball. Unlike Fanny, he is not cowed by Mansfield Park or its inhabitants, breezing in from his naval adventures to tell his experiences. He represents youth and buoyancy, and the vigorous world outside Northamptonshire society. He demonstrates, like Fanny and Susan, that 'nature' and not 'nurture' is the vital factor in a person's development. Coming from the dirty, disorganised Price household, with none of the advantages of Mansfield Park's young people, he nevertheless grows up happy, courageous, direct and personable.

Mr Price

At the lowest point of the novel's social spectrum, Mr Price represents not only poverty but lack of breeding as well. He is not lacking in capabilities, but has 'no curiosity, and no information beyond his profession'; reads 'only the newspaper and the navy-list' and talks only of dock-yard and harbour; worse, 'he swore and he drank, he was dirty and gross.' He is, in short, the diametric opposite of the urbane, authoritative, interesting and interested Sir Thomas. He would be in danger of being a caricature, were it not for the fact that when Mr Crawford arrives, he becomes 'a very different Mr Price in his behaviour to this most highly-respected stranger'. Although still not polished, his manners become 'more than passable: they were grateful, animated, manly: his expressions were those of an attached father, and a sensible man'. This change, though welcome to Fanny, is another sign of his dissimilarity to Sir Thomas, who behaves with the same innate good manners in society and at home.

The medium

The narrative

The point of view from which the story is told is generally that of a narrator who can see into the characters' minds and read their thoughts; who can see, too, how they behave in private, when nobody else is there (Fanny alone in the East room, for example). This narrator most frequently chooses to present Fanny's thoughts and emotions, though those of other characters are also revealed to us, particularly at moments of stress. The pattern of the narrative is the same for all the participants: their background and character are given before we hear them speak; their appearance is sketched in during their first 'scene'; throughout the action of the novel their behaviour and thoughts are assessed and reassessed, and in the final chapters their final fate is revealed, and the first causes of their actions given.

The narrative bears much of the story that one might expect to be conveyed by dialogue. The transfer of Edmund's love from Mary Crawford to Fanny is given in the narrator's words, not his, and we do not hear him proposing to Fanny. And indeed at the last, the narrator feigns to shy away from the close intimacy with the characters' emotions, and the power of disclosing them, that she (for it is, of course, Jane Austen herself) has enjoyed up to this point: there is happiness in Fanny's heart 'which no description can reach', however familiar with her the narrator may be.

Letters

Letter-writing plays an important part in the telling of *Mansfield Park*. Fanny, in coarse, uncivilised Portsmouth, hears of those she loves, of Mansfield and London, only through letters. Tom's illness, Henry Crawford's meeting Maria in London, the elopements, are all told through letters. The most revealing of all is the long letter (Chapter 45) in which Mary Crawford weighs up Edmund's prospects in the light of Tom's illness: we see, and understand, Fanny's disgust on reading this cold-blooded anticipation of a friend's death; the imputation too that Fanny would 'smile and look cunning', fancying that Mary Crawford had bribed the physician not to cure Tom, betrays a dark and sinister cast of thought. Edmund's long letter (Chapter 44) on the other hand – the letter expected and dreaded for so long – reveals an honest and transparent mind assessing and examining Mary Crawford and his own hopes with the comradeship that he shows in his conversations with Fanny; indeed where he can scarcely express emotions in speech, he can do so by letter.

Letters could separate, like Mrs Norris's 'angry' letter to Mrs Price on her marriage which kept the families estranged for years. They also more naturally formed a link. Fanny's early misery at Mansfield Park is epitomised by her inability to write to William: her first step towards happiness is taken when Edmund is sensitive enough to provide the means for her to write her letter.

Conversation

Three distinct kinds of conversation are to be found in *Mansfield Park*: the group conversation, the dialogue between two people, and the indirect speech. Most thoroughly and most originally explored in the novel is the group conversation, which we hear on many occasions such as when the theatricals are being planned and rehearsed, or the trip to Sotherton projected; or when during the game of Speculation, the conversation covers the cards, the new parsonage at Sotherton, and the sort of clergyman Edmund is going to be. Conversations among smaller groups also occur, such as the frequent talks between Mary Crawford, Edmund and Fanny, in which the two women take diametrically opposed views, with Edmund either taking a middle position or being staunchly defended by Fanny. Dialogues include the pensive confidences of Edmund and Fanny, the dangerous and cynical exchanges between the Crawfords and the low-toned flirtations of Henry Crawford and Maria. Indirect speech, a form at which Jane Austen particularly excelled, very often reports the lengthy utterances of Mrs Norris: 'Nobody loved plenty and hospitality more than herself – nobody more hated pitiful doings – the parsonage she believed had never been wanting in comforts of any sort, had never borne a bad character in *her time*, but this was a way of going on that she could not understand.'

Style

Narrative style

The narrative manner is as precise and analytical as the matter, its orderliness emphasised by the well-proportioned sentences, the balanced, antithetical clauses, the sequences of phrases. Only when events or emotions get out of hand does the syntax break down. In the comic passages the narrative, apparently innocuous, is laden with irony.

Balance

Balance, the predominant feature of the eighteenth-century prose writers admired by Jane Austen (such as Dr Johnson), is also predominant in *Mansfield Park*. Edmund's encouragement of Fanny is put antithetically: 'He had never knowingly given her pain, but he now felt that she required more positive kindness'; a measure is 'quite as welcome on one side, as it could be expedient on the other'. The antithetical form can make subtle points: Fanny 'grieved because she could not grieve'. It is also particularly suited to moral observations, and lends itself to aphorism: 'But there certainly are not so many men of large fortune in the world, as there are pretty women to deserve them.' These antitheses and opposites are in keeping with the system of contrasts running through the book.

Sequence

There are numerous examples of sequential sentences in which phrase is piled on phrase; at its simplest it may take a form such as 'she must . . . find consolation in fortune and consequence, bustle and the world.' It can also reach a very complex form in which enables Jane Austen to probe and analyse. Fanny's misfortunes when she first arrives at Mansfield Park are formally ordered and arranged in two sets of three: 'She was disheartened by Lady Bertram's silence, awed by Sir Thomas's grave looks, and quite overcome by Mrs Norris's admonitions. Her elder cousins mortified her by reflections on her size, and abashed her by noticing her shyness; Miss Lee wondered at her ignorance, and the maid-servants sneered at her clothes', the sentence culminating in the greatest misery of all: 'and when to these sorrows was added the idea of the brothers and sisters among whom she had always been important as play-fellow, instructress, and nurse, the despondence that sunk her little heart was severe.'

Dislocation

The calmly balanced narrative prose breaks up under emotional pressure just as a character's direct speech does (see 'Dislocation' in 'Style in speech' below, pp. 65–6). When Edmund tells Fanny about Mary Crawford, broken clauses and dashes appear: 'Sitting with her on Sunday evening – a wet Sunday evening – the very time of all others when if a friend is at hand the heart must be opened, and every thing told – no one else in the room, except his mother, who, after hearing an affecting sermon, had cried herself to sleep – it was impossible not to speak', and the narrative merges imperceptibly with indirect speech, of the same disjointed, unpolished kind. The narrative frequently expresses thought-patterns in a similar indirect and broken fashion, as Maria's thoughts when Henry Crawford is about to leave instead of proposing to her as she expects: 'He might talk of necessity, but she knew his independence. – The hand which had so pressed her's to his heart! – The hand and the heart were alike motionless and passive now!'

Narrative comedy

Mansfield Park is an extremely funny novel. In the narrative, as opposed to the spoken word (although of course in the novel both work together), the principal sources of amusement are comedy of situation, comedy of repetition, and comedy of inflection, in which the narrator's tone affects our reading.

Comedy of situation includes all those comic moments that are visual, such as the scene after Julia has burst in with news of her father's return and the actors are frozen, or when Sir Thomas finds Mr Yates 'a ranting young man, who appeared likely to knock him down backwards. At the very moment of Yates perceiving Sir Thomas,' he gives 'perhaps the very best start he had ever given in the whole course of his rehearsals'. Other moments include Lady Bertram asleep on the sofa while Tom explains that the theatricals will soothe her anxiety during her husband's absence; Julia, hot and out of breath, scrambling over the fence past the locked gate after Henry Crawford and Maria; Mrs Norris in the carriage clutching her pheasants' eggs.

Comedy of repetition is particularly marked; whereas Mr Rushworth and his blue dress and pink satin cloak are funny the first time they are mentioned, they become insidiously funnier each subsequent time, like the green baize curtain, and Lady Bertram on her sofa with her pug.

The narrator's dry tone enhances all the comic moments of the novel: the inflection may depend only on a single word, as 'kindly' in Agatha's attentions to Mr Rushworth: 'she very kindly took his part in hand, and curtailed every speech that admitted being shortened'; or Mr Norris, 'so terribly haunted by these ideas in the sad solitariness of her cottage, as to be obliged to take daily refuge in the dining room of the park', where 'dining room' encapsulates the joke.

Narrative irony

Irony may be classified as irony of situation, irony of narrative tone, and the irony of transcribing the characters' speeches or actions without comment, in all the ridiculousness which they themselves do not perceive. The essence of irony is that the dupe does not see things as they are, whereas the onlooker does. Edmund's idea that he can elevate Mary Crawford from her worldliness and frivolity is doomed to be unsuccessful; we can hear from her words, both to Edmund himself, and even more to her brother Henry, that she is corrupt; but poor Edmund is blinded by tenderness and sentiment. In Henry Crawford's case the irony lies in the reversal of the situation; having planned to spend a fortnight 'making Fanny Price in love with me' he is spurred by her resistance into becoming 'in love, very much in love' himself instead.

Fanny is not aware of the ironic fact known to Sir Thomas and suggested to the reader, that she will soon be 'heartily sick' of the home for which she cherishes such romantic ideals.

The narrative tone can be savagely ironic: Maria is 'prepared for matrimony by an hatred of home, restraint, and tranquillity; by the misery of disappointed affection, and contempt of the man she was to marry'. It may, however, be mild: '[Fanny] seemed to have the little wood all to herself. She could almost have thought, that Edmund and Miss Crawford had left it, but that it was impossible for Edmund to forget her so entirely.' The acuteness of a single word can often throw a whole passage back upon itself; when Mary Crawford speaks kindly to Fanny after Mrs Norris's attack on her for not taking part in the theatricals, she tries to raise her spirits, and, 'by a look at her brother, she prevented any further entreaty from the theatrical board, and the really good feelings by which she was almost purely governed, were rapidly restoring her to all the little she had lost in Edmund's favour'. The word 'almost' here demolishes her kindness and reveals her motives remorselessly.

Style in speech

Balance and sequence
The characters in *Mansfield Park* speak almost as formally as the narrator, in polished periods that only break up at times of stress. Even speaking lightly, they pronounce aphorisms, such as Henry Crawford's 'An engaged woman is always more agreeable than a disengaged,' or Mary Crawford's 'every body should marry as soon as they can do it to advantage.' The best example of formal speech is that of Sir Thomas, who speaks in balanced, sequential sentences, as can be seen in Chapter 1 in his assessment of the implications of having Fanny Price to live with them. When later in the book he is pressing Mr Crawford's cause, he employs a similar sequential system, presenting a young man 'with every thing to recommend him; not merely situation in life, fortune, and character, but with more than common agreeableness, with address and conversation pleasing to every body'.

Dislocation
Not all the characters can keep their syntax intact under pressure as Sir Thomas can. Edmund, who generally speaks as measuredly as his father, loses track of his sentences when he tries to tell Fanny (Chapter 47) about his last talk with Mary Crawford. He speaks in broken phrases, without main verbs, never finishing his sentences: 'Guess what I must have felt. To hear the woman whom – no harsher name than folly given! – So voluntarily, so freely, so coolly to canvass it! – No

reluctance, no horror, no feminine – shall I say? No modest loathings! – This is what the world does.'

Jane Austen also uses disjointed and unfinished sentences in entirely different circumstances in group speech, such as the conglomerate hubbub of interrupted remarks while the play is being chosen: 'on one side or the other it was a continual repetition of, "Oh; no, *that* will never do. Let us have no ranting tragedies. Too many characters – Not a tolerable woman's part in the play – Any thing but *that*, my dear Tom. It would be impossible to fill it up – One could not expect any body to take such a part – Nothing but buffoonery from beginning to end."'

Comedy in speech
The comedy of the speech in *Mansfield Park* lies in the sheer ridiculousness of some of the characters' words, often accentuated by repetition, either of ideas or of words: Lady Bertram's insistent 'I sent Chapman to dress her, you know' as the cause of Fanny's success; everyone in the Price household bringing the news that the *Thrush* has left harbour; Mrs Norris's catchphrase 'I must keep a spare room for a friend.' Mrs Norris also excels in the long speech which grows funnier and funnier as it goes on, such as her conversation during the return from Sotherton (Chapter 10), her discourse on the making of the green baize curtain and the vanquishing of the carpenter's son (Chapter 15), or the story of how she made Maria's match with Mr Rushworth, which uses the same kind of ludicrous juxtaposition, concluding: 'I could not bear to sit at my ease, and be dragged up at the expense of those noble animals. I caught a dreadful cold, but *that* I did not regard. My object was accomplished in the visit.'

Part 4

Hints for study

Patterns

Look for patterns in the novel. *Mansfield Park* can be divided very easily into separate episodes, separate groupings of its characters, and separate stages in Fanny's development. These may coincide, but not necessarily always. All are very dependent on background, which you should consider in detail. Patterns of the relationships between the major characters also change, affected by these episodes, groupings and stages. The patterns of relationships are particularly interesting in their contrasting or parallel courses; again, each can be affected by some other relationship. There is also a pattern in the characters themselves which can be discerned, again by parallel or by contrast: Lady Bertram and her two sisters; Edmund in direct contrast with Henry Crawford, Mr Yates a paler copy of the latter with a parallel career in the novel. Lady Bertram and her two sisters are constantly compared and contrasted. Some of the sections in Part 3 will help you to look out for such patterns, but you will also find many others for yourself.

Episodes

The major episodes in *Mansfield Park* are: the trip to Sotherton (Chapters 8–10); the theatricals (Chapters 13–18); Henry Crawford's wooing of Fanny (Chapters 24–36); Fanny in Portsmouth (Chapters 38–46). Surrounding these we find preparatory or transitional passages: after Chapters 1–2, Fanny's earliest days at Mansfield Park, comes the assembling of the characters, Maria's engagement and the preparations for visiting Sotherton; Chapters 11–12 are transitional, showing life at Mansfield Park in Sir Thomas's absence but before the theatricals; after the theatricals and Sir Thomas's return, Chapters 19–23 are again transitional, showing the house settling back into its accustomed order; Chapter 37, after Mr Crawford's proposal, prepares for Fanny's trip to Portsmouth by showing Sir Thomas's intentions and Fanny's expectations; Chapters 47–8 concludes all the plots developed in the episodes.

Grouping

The early chapters show Fanny as isolated from the main group of Mansfield Park characters, though linked to them by Edmund. As further persons arrive, the group is essentially the Bertram family with Mr Rushworth loosely attached to it through his engagement to Maria (Chapters 3–7), with the Grants and the Crawfords in easy communication with them, and Fanny still on the outside, linked only by her friendship with Edmund. At Sotherton, a kaleidoscopic regrouping takes place: Henry Crawford, at first vacillating between Julia and Maria, plumps for Maria, thus displacing Mr Rushworth; Edmund is openly associated with Mary Crawford for the first time, thus altering Fanny's link with the main group, though from this point until Chapter 46 we often see Fanny, Mary Crawford and Edmund as a trio separated from the others. Up to the middle of the theatricals, Fanny, Julia and Edmund are separated from the main company; when Edmund agrees to act (Chapter 16) he is absorbed into the larger group; Mrs Norris is part of it, Lady Bertram benignly on its fringe. Sir Thomas's return breaks the theatrical grouping and re-establishes the small circle of Mansfield Park, reduced by the absence of Maria, Mr Rushworth and Julia, and by Sir Thomas's 'drawing back from intimacies in general'. Eventually the Crawfords and Grants rejoin the Mansfield circle, and as Edmund's links with Miss Crawford strengthen, Mr Crawford approaches Fanny, now much more at the centre of the Mansfield group. When he proposes and the rest of the group try to persuade Fanny to marry him, we see the two of them linked in people's eyes – this is the first time they have linked Fanny with anyone. The sudden shift to Portsmouth isolates Fanny again (apart from her momentary warm feeling for Mr Crawford during his visit). Her alienation from her Portsmouth family is almost as complete as her alienation by distance from those at Mansfield Park and from the secondary group of characters in London – Maria, Julia, Mr Rushworth, Mr Yates, Mary Crawford and eventually Henry Crawford. The last but one chapter integrates Fanny completely into the Mansfield Park group; the last unites her with Edmund, and splits off in twos the disturbers of harmony (Maria with Mr Crawford, then with Mrs Norris; Julia with Mr Yates), leaving the core of the Mansfield Park family intact and close-knit. An awareness of these shifting groupings is vital (and happily inescapable) in reading *Mansfield Park*.

Stages in Fanny's development

The novel traces Fanny's development from immaturity, lack of self-knowledge and reticence, towards maturity, self-knowledge and confidence. From her early timidity (Chapters 1–2) she is helped by Edmund's education of her mind and taste; but it is important to notice that as she grows up she stays fixed in a childish timidity for a long time, hence Sir Thomas's reproof that William 'must find his sister at sixteen in some respects too much like his sister at ten' (Chapter 3). An important step in Fanny's growth to maturity is taken when she acknowledges to herself her tender feelings for Edmund (Chapter 4) and although this brings her increasing sadness when she sees him with Mary Crawford (Chapters 7–36), the recognition of this sadness is in itself a stage in self-knowledge. Another part of herself which Fanny accepts and develops is her power of observation, which she employs at Sotherton (Chapter 10) and during the theatricals (especially Chapters 14–18). Her resolute refusal to act shows her increasing moral strength; her new ability to talk to Sir Thomas (Chapter 21) and her sense of being more important at Mansfield Park are further stages, culminating in her 'coming out ball', when she 'comes out' into individuality as well as into society. It is this individuality and independence that are noticed by the experienced Mr Crawford, and that attract him; Fanny's refusal of his proposal marks full self-confidence. The final step in her own self-knowledge is her admission to herself at Portsmouth that Mansfield is her home, and her true society (Chapter 39). Fortified by this and by Edmund's awakening to a realisation of Miss Crawford's character, she can go back to Mansfield Park to assert her own good sense and comfort the family, earning her right to a place, a home and a husband there.

Patterns in relationships

Every new person that appears in this highly patterned novel alters the design. Relationships within the same family can vary widely. Sir Thomas, for example, has very different relationships with the lovely, indolent Lady Bertram; with the over-active Mrs Norris; with his two dissimilar sons; with his daughters, whom he finds he hardly knows. His relationship with Fanny is of perpetual interest, impeded at first by his stern dignity and her timidity; they are drawn closer on his return from the West Indies by his approval and her interest in his conversation (and her new prettiness), until his surprised disapproval of her refusal to marry Henry Crawford separates them again. He is stern and cold, and as 'master in his house' must be obeyed when he determines that she should go to Portsmouth, knowing her well enough to guess that she will be repelled by it. The correctness of his judgement about this, and hers about the Crawfords, reunite them. The steps in the relationships between each character and the others are plain to see: follow each step by step and you will find that the strands knit together to an intricate and unified whole.

Settings

The background to each scene of *Mansfield Park* is vital, not merely for 'local colour' but to reveal character, emotions, relationships. The trip to Sotherton, as has been pointed out above, is of great significance; but how many different aspects of it are catalysts to the story! The approach to the house shows Maria's materialism, her momentary pride in the house, her sense of possession as she details the cottages, alms-houses, oaks, and so on; the different parts of the estate, park, drive, avenue, wood and wilderness tempt different characters in different ways – Maria and Henry Crawford are drawn out through the locked iron gate into the park, Edmund and Mary Crawford to the shade of the fine trees. The chapel reveals many things – via its altar-rail Mary Crawford learns for the first time that Edmund is going to be a clergyman; its lack of ornament induces Fanny to reveal her yearning for romantic arches, inscriptions and banners. It shows Maria about to be united with Mr Rushworth but flirting with Mr Crawford; it shows the erosion of tradition in the Rushworth household, the loss of family prayers being the equivalent of the loss of the fine oaks felled to 'improve' the estate.

The Price household is a very striking setting, in its bustle, dirt and noise; Fanny's escape to fresh air on the battlements with Henry Crawford projects a new idea, of compatibility with him outside the claustrophobic confines of the Price house. Other backgrounds are equally memorable: the room used as a theatre, Fanny's beloved East room, the parsonage and its shrubbery, all inspiring incidents and confidences, and above all, Mansfield Park itself, informing the novel with its physical presence.

Character and characterisation

The characters in *Mansfield Park* are diverse, but illuminating in their contrasting natures. Mary Crawford's worldly frivolity shows up Fanny's sincerity and depth in almost every conversation they have, and in all the conversations each has with Edmund. Fanny's character is revealed by the contrast with Maria and Julia, apparently so superior to her in looks and accomplishments, her reticence a commentary on their confidence, her conduct when besieged by Henry Crawford so different from theirs. Edmund and Henry Crawford show up each other's different qualities as do Edmund and Tom. Certain less obvious contrasts can also be noted such as that between William and Henry Crawford, the former poor, hard-working, fresh, sincere and steady, the latter rich, idle, jaded, insincere and inconstant. Look for revealing comparisons such as these; for example in Lady Bertram and her sisters, in Maria· and Julia. Look too for characters who are like each other;

Henry and Mary Crawford, Edmund and Fanny, William and Fanny, who reveal sides of themselves through that likeness, and also because they can speak openly to each other.

Character is revealed in *Mansfield Park* by what the characters say themselves, by what other characters say about them, and by the acute analysis offered by the narrator, which is usually given first before the character ever utters a word in our hearing, frequently revised or restated throughout the novel, and finalised in the last two chapters, when not only everyone's subsequent careers, but also their motives in the present plot are revealed. (See 'Conversation' and 'Narrative' in Part 3, section on 'The medium', for examples. You will find many others in the novel).

Chapters for intensive study

There are certain key chapters which can usefully be studied, falling into the categories of 'episodes', 'regroupings' and 'stages in Fanny's development'. Study them, consider how each is prepared for, and look at its effect on the subsequent course of the novel: Fanny's arrival at Mansfield Park (Chapter 2); the scene in the chapel at Sotherton (Chapter 9); the passing of the iron gate (Chapter 10); the theatricals, especially the two chapters leading up to the final rehearsal (Chapters 17–18); the game of Speculation (Chapter 25); Fanny's first days in Portsmouth (Chapter 38–9).

Some sample questions

(1) Discuss the point of view of the narrator in *Mansfield Park*.

(2) How far can the characters of *Mansfield Park* be said to be divided into those who are active and those who are passive, and how useful is this distinction in our view of the novel as a whole?

(3) Comment on the contrasting of fantasy and reality in *Mansfield Park*.

(4) 'A modest degree of materialism is essential to a well-regulated life.' Is this a lesson to be learnt from *Mansfield Park*?

(5) Comment on the significance of the 'theatricals' in *Mansfield Park*.

(6) Discuss the importance of time in *Mansfield Park*.

(7) In what way can the settings of *Mansfield Park* be said to be an intrinsic part of the novel, and not merely a background to it?

(8) Of the many lessons that Fanny Price learns at Mansfield Park, 'Know thyself' is the hardest for her to master.

(9) Outline and comment on three or four narrative techniques in *Mansfield Park*.

(10) Discuss the pattern of Fanny Price's relationships.

(11) Consider roles and role-playing in *Mansfield Park*.

(12) Can the structure of *Mansfield Park* be said to be symmetrical?

(13) Discuss Jane Austen's skill in grouping her characters, as seen in *Mansfield Park*.

---

(10) Discuss the pattern of Fanny Price's relationships.

Fanny's principal relationships fall into two different patterns: those with Henry and Mary Crawford are circular and closing; those with William, Sir Thomas and Lady Bertram, Susan and above all Edmund are continuous, expanding, capable of infinite growth. Her relationship with Henry Crawford starts in mistrust, as she worries about his harmful attentions to Maria and Julia. Next, she is scandalised by his escapade at Sotherton, when he and Maria cross the iron gate. The distance between Fanny and Henry Crawford lessens when she begins to admire his acting and his reading, and he resolves first to make her love him, then, thinking himself 'in love, very much in love', to persuade her to marry him. At the time of his proposal, she is aware of his kindness, and grateful for his exertions to promote William's career, but finds his attentions unpleasant. After refusing him, she resists pressure from others, claiming that he and she are too different to marry. In Portsmouth, they come as close together as is possible for them, given their natures. She is impressed with the contrast between him and the members of her own family there; she also considers him more upright and responsible than before. She begins to think that if she were to marry him, she would have a home to offer Susan. Just as she seemed on the point of yielding and taking part in the theatricals, so now she seems to be yielding to him. Finally, at second hand, she hears of his elopement with Maria, which vindicates her original mistrust of him and confirms her belief that he is corrupt. Their relationship has returned to its starting-point.

Fanny's relationship with Mary Crawford is also circular, starting with mistrust and disapproval of her indecorous conversation, and progressing to fear of her effect on Edmund, and alienation from her as she usurps Fanny's place as his companion. Following Mary Crawford's kindness to Fanny when Mrs Norris insults her for refusing to act in the play, a strange relationship develops between Edmund, Mary Crawford and Fanny, often apparent in three-sided discussions. When Edmund is away, a curious intimacy grows between the two women, Fanny feeling compelled to visit Miss Crawford by 'a kind of fascination'; on his return, Edmund professes himself delighted by the friendship between the two beings most dear to him. Fanny's disillusionment with Mary Crawford is caused by the latter's letters to Portsmouth, especially that wishing for Tom's death. Fanny returns to her early dislike and disapproval, vindicated by Mary Crawford's betrayal of her own amorality in her last interview with Edmund.

Fanny's other relationships are neither closed nor circular. That with William expands as brother and sister become closer and happier together as they grow older; the same promises for Susan. Her relationships with Sir Thomas and Lady Bertram develop from her early fear and reticence into love and trust, the only setback the estrangement caused by Sir Thomas's anger when she refuses Henry Crawford. The most expansive of all Fanny's relationships is that with Edmund, constant and steady, unharmed even by his infatuation with Mary Crawford. It blossoms from a relationship of pupil and teacher to that of true equals; Fanny's love for him, acknowledged in her heart near the beginning of the novel, is matched by his for her at its end.

---

(12) Can the structure of *Mansfield Park* be said to be symmetrical?

The structure of the novel is not symmetrical but purposely asymmetrical. It cannot be cut up into equal or balancing sections: it can be divided into sections, but these do not balance each other neatly. One such division would be into three sections: the gathering of the characters and build-up to the theatricals; the theatricals themselves; and the post-theatrical period. This is satisfactory on some levels, showing Mansfield Park in its usual order; then disrupted by the play; then back in order after Sir Thomas's return. It also makes a pattern for Fanny's development within her society; in the first part she is in the background; during the theatricals, though not acting, she is brought more to the centre of attention; and after the theatricals she is in the foreground – more of an individual, more important to Mansfield Park in the absence of Maria and Julia. But even such a classification is neither balanced nor symmetrical, as the theatricals take place in the first third of the novel, and not at its centre (Chapters 13–18 out of 48).

Nor can the novel be forced into a rigid symmetry by looking at it 'episodically'. There is a certain pattern of episodes with transition passages between them: Fanny's early life and the gathering of the characters leading up to the Sotherton episode (Chapters 8–10); a regrouping transition (Chapters 11–12) leading to the theatricals (Chapter 13–18); Fanny's transition to importance (Chapters 19–23) leading to the Henry Crawford episode (Chapters 24–36); a transition chapter (37) leading to her stay in Portsmouth (Chapters 38–46), with the two final chapters tying up the ends. But, as can be seen, the episodes are of unequal length, and are not meant to 'balance' each other.

It would be false, however, to impose a symmetrical pattern on the novel. Its structure is linear, showing a consistent movement forward in Fanny's development, and its 'lines' are not artificially rigid. Just as the theatricals are abortive, and tail off without a performance, so the plots and sub-plots are snatched from us, never reaching their dénouement under our eyes. Their ends are tied up for us off-stage, their conclusions sketched in for us in the final chapters. The novel's interest comes from the dynamic tension *before* they are resolved: the resolution is perfunctory. The novel's balance comes from its intricate web of parallels and contrasts, and its movement towards harmony: it has not, and does not need, a formally symmetrical framework.

---

(13) Discuss Jane Austen's skill in grouping her characters, as seen in *Mansfield Park*.

If we think of Fanny as an individual moving gradually towards her place in society, we can see at any point in the novel how close she has come to that place. The early parts of the book are full of memorable images showing how far from it she is; the little girl in tears on the attic staircase (approached by Edmund, thus establishing a new group of two); or the young woman looking down at the happy riding party, able to hear its 'sound of merriment' but quite cut off from it. At the time of the theatricals, we see Fanny and Julia as 'two solitary sufferers' withdrawn from the acting group, but on opposite sides and unconnected with each other. At times during this period the actual physical grouping of the characters is very striking: as when Fanny is under pressure to act from the others at the tea-table, presided over by Mrs Norris. Mary Crawford, 'with some feelings of resentment and mortification' at Edmund's refusal to play Anhalt, has just 'moved her chair considerably nearer the tea-table', but when Mrs Norris insults Fanny, she changes the grouping: ' "I do not like my situation; this *place* is too hot for me" – and moved away from her chair to the opposite side of the table close to Fanny'.

Grouping may also have ironic implications, as when we see Edmund, Mary Crawford and Fanny apparently grouped together some way apart from the rest, in deceptive intimacy. This kind of apparent grouping is also evident when Henry Crawford visits Fanny at Portsmouth, and they appear temporarily to be 'paired' in the foreground, with the unpolished society of Portsmouth just behind, and the rest of the characters far away at Mansfield and in London. Fanny is soon alone again, until the penultimate chapter when she returns to Mansfield Park as a fully integrated, effective member of its society; in the last chapter we learn that she and Edmund are united in the closer grouping of marriage within that society.

This overall pattern of grouping is fundamental to the novel; there are also very distinct and memorable groupings in individual scenes. The placing during the game of Speculation, for example, is brought to our notice, with Henry Crawford between Lady Bertram and Fanny, Mary Crawford in competitive isolation in the game, with cross-groupings as Henry Crawford and Edmund talk about the latter's new parsonage, with Mary Crawford equally alienated from that discussion. The groupings and regroupings at Sotherton are also charted in detail, culminating in the period when Fanny, left on the bench by Edmund and Mary Crawford, becomes a point of convergence and then divergence for other groupings: Maria, Mr Rushworth and Henry Crawford arrive at her bench before splitting up, Mr Rushworth to go back to the house, the other two to move outwards beyond the locked gate. Subsequently Julia and Mr Rushworth, separately, arrive at this point before following them. Fanny, observant of their dramas, conscious of her own, is the central point.

Both the overall pattern of grouping and the individual momentary groupings are of the utmost importance in Mansfield Park: the physical grouping represents the inner feelings of the characters, and their relationships to each other and to society as a whole.

Part 5

Suggestions for further reading

The text

The text of *Mansfield Park* used in these notes is that of the Penguin English Library, edited with an introduction by Tony Tanner, Penguin Books, Harmondsworth, 1966, many times reprinted.

Other novels by Jane Austen

Sense and Sensibility, The Oxford Illustrated Jane Austen, 3rd edition, Oxford University Press, London, 1965.
Pride and Prejudice, The Oxford Illustrated Jane Austen, revised edition, Oxford University Press, London, 1965.
Emma, The Oxford Illustrated Jane Austen, revised edition, Oxford University Press, London, 1978.
Northanger Abbey and *Persuasion*, The Oxford Illustrated Jane Austen, revised edition, Oxford University Press, London, 1969.

These are all edited by R. W. Chapman, with informative introductions and notes. These novels also appear in the Oxford English Novels series, and in the Penguin English Library.

Juvenilia, unfinished works, letters

Juvenilia, Early Work, and *Fragments*; *Lady Susan*; *The Watsons*; *Sanditon* are all reprinted in *Minor Works*, The Oxford Illustrated Jane Austen, Vol. VI, Oxford University Press, London, 1954.
Lady Susan; *The Watsons*; *Sanditon* appear also in the Penguin English Library, Penguin Books, Harmondsworth, 1966.
Jane Austen's Letters, ed. R. W. Chapman, Oxford University Press, London, revised edition, 1959.

The Life of Jane Austen

AUSTEN-LEIGH, JAMES: *A Memoir of Jane Austen*, 2nd edition, London, Bentley, 1871. The first biography of Jane Austen, written by her nephew. It contains interesting family details.

CECIL, DAVID: *A Portrait of Jane Austen*, Constable, London, 1978; Penguin Books, Harmondsworth, 1980. A delightful illustrated account of Jane Austen's life and family.

CRAIK, W. A.: *Jane Austen in her time*, Nelson, London, 1969. An illuminating record of life in Jane Austen's time, with illustrated details of houses, furniture, the daily round.

LASKI, MARGHANITA: *Jane Austen and Her World*, Thames and Hudson, London, 1969. Splendid pictures of Jane Austen and her times.

Books about Jane Austen's work

CRAIK, W. A.: *Jane Austen. The Six Novels*, University Paperbacks Series, Methuen, London, 1965. Excellent on characterisations and style.

DUCKWORTHY, ALISTAIR M.: *The Improvement of the Estate*, Johns Hopkins Press, Baltimore and London, 1971. A good account of the culture and morality of the time, with special reference to houses and estates, and therefore particularly relevant to a study of *Mansfield Park*.

FLEISCHMAN, ANN: *A Reading of Mansfield Park. An Essay in Critical Synthesis*, University of Minnesota Press, Minneapolis, 1967. Specifically about *Mansfield Park*.

HARDY, BARBARA: *A Reading of Jane Austen*, Peter Owen, London, 1975. Sensitive criticism of Jane Austen's work, particularly good on *Mansfield Park*.

HODGE, JANE AIKEN: *The Double Life of Jane Austen*, Hodder & Stoughton, London, Sydney, Auckland, Toronto, 1972. A good treatment of Jane Austen, with an interesting section on *Mansfield Park*.

PINION, F. B.: *A Jane Austen Companion*, Macmillan (St Martin's Press), London and Basingstoke, 1973. A critical survey and reference book: an excellent guide to the social conventions of the time, with a glossary of out-of-date words and a good bibliography.

SHERRY, NORMAN: *Jane Austen*. 'Literature in Perspective' Series, Evans Bros., London, 1966. Good on the background and literary methods of Jane Austen.

SOUTHAM, B. C. (ED.): *Jane Austen. The Critical Heritage*, Routledge & Kegan Paul, London; Barnes & Noble, New York, 1968. A comprehensive collection of criticism of Jane Austen.

WRIGHT, ANDREW H.: *Jane Austen's Novels: a Study in Structure*, Pelican Books, Harmondsworth, 1972. A handy guide to the novels and to Jane Austen's themes and materials.

Collections including articles on Mansfield Park

HALPERIN, JOHN (ED.): *Jane Austen Bicentenary Essays*, Cambridge University Press, Cambridge, London, New York, Melbourne, 1975.

SOUTHAM, B. C. (ED.): *Jane Austen: Sense and Sensibility, Pride and Prejudice and Mansfield Park. A Casebook*, Macmillan, London and Basingstoke, 1976.

WATT, IAN (ED.): *Jane Austen. A collection of Critical Essays*, Prentice-Hall Inc., Englewood Cliffs, N. J., 1963.

The author of these notes

BARBARA HAYLEY was educated at Trinity College Dublin. After a business career in London she took a PhD in English and American Literature at the University of Kent at Canterbury and lectured at Cambridge University as a Fellow of Lucy Cavendish College. She is now a lecturer in English at St Patrick's College, Maynooth, the National University of Ireland. Her books include *The Carleton Bibliography*; *William Carleton and the Nineteenth Century Anglo-Irish Tradition*; *An Appendix to Carleton's Traits and Stories*. She is also author of York Notes on Sean O'Casey's *Juno and the Paycock* and Jane Austen's *Emma*.

York Handbooks: list of titles

York Handbooks form a companion series to York Notes and are designed to meet the wider needs of students of English and related fields. Each volume is a compact study of a given subject area, written by an authority with experience in communicating the essential ideas to students at all levels.

A DICTIONARY OF LITERARY TERMS (Second Edition)
by MARTIN GRAY

ENGLISH POETRY
by CLIVE T. PROBYN

AN INTRODUCTION TO LINGUISTICS
by LORETO TODD

STUDYING SHAKESPEARE
by MARTIN STEPHEN *and* PHILIP FRANKS